SAS AND

SELF DEFENCE

Barry Davies BEM

HarperCollins*Publishers*

HarperCollins Publishers

Westerhill Rd, Bishopbriggs Glasgow G64 2QT

www.**fire**and**water**.co.uk

First published 2001

Reprint 10 9 8 7 6 5 4 3 2 1 0

© Barry Davies 2001

ISBN 0 00 710231 3

Technical Adviser: Steve Collins

Photo Credits: all photography © PS5, except for images on pp. 21, 28, 42, 43, 51, 56, 146, 165, 169, 170, 172, 176, 187, 189, 199, 201, 210, © PhotoDisc 2001; on pp. 38, 45, 53, 57, © Artville 2001; on pp. 26, 31, 39, 46, 47, 54, 205 © Barry Davies; and on pp. 196, 197, © The Printer's Devil

Material in this book first appeared in the
Collins Gem *SAS Self-defence*

Printed in Hong Kong by Midas

WARNING

CONTENTS

Defensive moves

Attacks on women

Protecting your property

Vehicle safety

Travel

Medical emergencies

INTRODUCTION

We would be very lucky indeed to live out our lives without any injury to our bodies. The world is a dangerous place, but humans have learnt to adapt. We shelter from the elements, most of our environment is free of wild beasts, rigidly enforced safety laws protect us from physical damage. Despite all this, as we enter the new millennium, our biggest enemy is still another human being. No matter how advanced the human race becomes, the aggression factor remains with us. It is not unique to the individual, the whole world at some stage has participated in violence, and continues to do so. Wars, famine, terrorism daily fill our television screens. Normally, unless one is a member of the armed forces, we do not become involved, but even at home, protected by a solid police force, are we really that safe? If you live in London, your chances of being attacked, or having your home burgled, are better than one in four.

Here are two headlines from recent newspapers: 'Baby's hands and feet chopped off': A French mother returned to her home to discover that the baby sitter had mutilated her child; the baby died subsequently. 'Jail for mugger of DDP husband': A member of a teenage gang stabbed and nearly killed the husband of the Director of Public Prosecutions.

How do we deal with such situations? It is not easy, but I have called on all my experience gained serving for 18 years in the SAS. The SAS are renowned world-wide for working in violent areas and are trained to cope with the most desperate situations. Adapting SAS methods and philosophy to self-defence is common sense and I have tried to illustrate the SAS's techniques in this book so that they apply to every age, and to both sexes.

You must not treat street fighting as a game, or as a sport where the Marquess of Queensberry rules apply. There are no rules – other than to escape or minimise the injury to yourself or those with you. You must also understand that fighting can cause damage to either side, and perhaps result even in death. Defending yourself and others is your basic right but whatever reasonable force you use to defend yourself must be justified – and that justification may be challenged by a court of law. There is no justification for introducing violence into a confrontation, other than when you or others are directly threatened by violence. In short, self-defence techniques should only be used for self-defence purposes and you must stay within the law.

This sounds bad, and you will ask yourself, how am I to defend myself? For a start, most fights last a very short time, the majority no longer than 30 seconds. Therefore, if you are fit, take responsibility for yourself, and prepare your defence in advance, you can win. But before you get involved in fighting, consider avoiding the situation altogether: there is no guarantee that your self-defence skills will always work because your opponent may be quicker and stronger than you (few pick on anyone larger than themselves) and indeed, may also posses martial arts knowledge. Also, I believe it is possible to view 'self-defence' more broadly than in terms of dealing with attacks against the person. The same mental attitudes and preparedness that will hopefully minimise the effects of any physical assault can also be applied to other areas of potential danger in your life. For this reason, the book will discuss ways to handle threats to your property and against you from sources other than personal attack.

Barry Davies

The Problem

BECOME AWARE OF VIOLENCE

We have all observed a rabbit in the wild; for the most part all we get is a quick flash as the animal scurries from view into the hedgerow or down its burrow. Have you ever asked yourself why they run off at the first sight of a human? It's because they are afraid. This fear makes them constantly aware of their surroundings, alerting them to any intruder. For most of us, the only animal we fear is another human. Self-defence starts with you being as alert to danger as a rabbit. In order to defend ourselves against our fellow man we need to be aware of our surroundings and alert to the possibility of attack. Unfortunately most attackers plan their assault, choosing their victim and preparing the ground to facilitate success. In choosing their victim they will look for someone who is weaker than them, or they will use a weapon to give them an advantage. They will choose an isolated spot, or attack when the victim is alone.

It is advisable to put violence into proper perspective: for every person that is murdered in the United Kingdom, five more die on the road, while two hundred die each year from smoking. Nevertheless, violent crime is on the increase, and the first thing

you must do is keep your eyes open. If you are aware that violence can take place anywhere and at any time then your chances of avoiding it are greatly increased.

Spotting trouble before it begins is the best way of avoiding it. For example, if you get on the Underground and find that half-way through your journey your carriage is invaded by drunken football hooligans, simply get off and either get in another carriage, or wait for the next tube. If you find yourself the target of aggression in, say, a pub, simply leave. It is always easy to perceive the threat to be greater than it really is. On the whole, Britain is a fairly safe place and the bulk of the population is fairly law-abiding. We become used to our own daily routine, we meet the same people most days either at work, out shopping or at home. This fosters in us a sense of leading a normal life, and it's only when we step outside our own normal routine that we tend to take notice. For example, people who live in the countryside and travel to a large city often feel vulnerable – at such times the mind will automatically tell you to be aware.

UNDERSTAND THE SITUATION IN ADVANCE

If you are drinking in a pub, and you see two drunks arguing, it is unlikely that you will join in. The reason is that you have spotted the danger and will wish to distance yourself from it. Unfortunately, there may be times when the danger against you is planned by someone who has a grudge against you, or when you are simply a victim of a random crime.

Most drunken incidents can be spotted well in advance and thus avoided. However, planned crimes are usually well hidden. Criminals will normally wait in dark and quiet places: parks, backstreets, alleyways. Plan your route in advance to avoid such places. Walk where the street lighting is good, and remember that increasingly, town centres are monitored by closed-circuit cameras linked to the police.

Understanding that you may get hurt, and taking steps to avoid potentially dangerous situations, is called planning and preparation. This is something the SAS are very good at. Before they go out on any operation, where they may encounter the enemy, they study, they equip and they plan for contingencies.

There is no reason why everyone should not adopt this same attitude for everyday life.

WHO IS, AND WHAT MOTIVATES, YOUR ATTACKER?

The odds are that your attacker will be between 16 and 28 years of age, male and unemployed. His main motivations will be money, envy, drunkenness or drugs, and in some cases, sexual. It is vital to discern what your attacker is after, and what the threat to you actually is. If, for example, you are stopped by a street mugger, he may just want your valuables before disappearing. On the other hand, a rapist will want a lot more before he sees fit to let you go – and then it's a risk giving in.

CONFIDENTLY ASSERT YOURSELF

Confidence shows through your body movement, your language, and your eye-to-eye contact. Humans are animals, and like all animals, large or small, we all learn to recognise whether our foe is stronger or weaker than ourselves. Walking briskly along at a keen pace sends out a better signal than just sauntering along with a set of head-phones on. If you are in an unknown city, try walking with the crowd, or by the side of someone as if you are together. How you dress is part of your individuality, but try not to stand out too much. If you're dressing up for a night out, especially if you're wearing high heels or restrictive clothing, arrange for a taxi home or travel in a group. If someone challenges you,

➤   Stand in an alert position.
➤   Listen to what your opponent is saying.
➤   Look them straight in the eye and hold the contact.

There are two reasons for doing this: (a) to make an assessment of your opponent, and (b) to show him what he has to deal with.

AUTHOR'S NOTE

➤   I have often found that it is better to say very little when confronted by any would-be assailant. A quiet and relaxed stance can have a dramatic effect. At the first sign that your assailant is backing down break the confrontation and remove yourself.

(contd)

15

➤ Don't worry about abuse being hurled at your back, but do listen for movement if he decides to chase you(contd)

YOUR BODY LANGUAGE

Body language, and how we dress, express much about the individual.
Clothes, dress sense and accessories give away much about who we are; for example, a uniform of some description normally indicates certain types of authority – police, soldier, nurse, traffic warden, etc. Anyone wearing a smart suit and carrying a briefcase will normally be classed as a business person. Next time you walk down the street, try guessing what people do for a living only in the broadest sense, i.e. businessperson, tourist, factory worker and so on. You will be surprised to learn that you will be correct in most cases. While you are doing this, assess

your own body language. How do people view you? Do you walk with a spring in your step? Does your dress style say 'I'm neat and tidy, but not flashy rich'? Do you look fit? By doing this you are becoming aware. Unfortunately, aggression and strength are the two main factors which normally decide the outcome of any conflict, but with awareness, surprise and confidence your deterrent factor is greatly improved. Protecting yourself against physical attack is a natural reaction.

ANALYSE YOUR DAILY ROUTINE

It is so simple to slip into a routine: we get up, we go to work, we come home, we go down the pub. There is nothing wrong with this, and in our own local environment, it can prove to have many advantages. For example, if the old lady at number 24 has not been seen for a few days or the milk is piling up, someone will notice because a routine has been broken.

The danger starts when we are out of our normal environment and the familiar routines don't exist. The problem then is how to detect when a threat exists? The answer is simple: when you feel threatened. Under normal circumstances, your body will always react to danger. Fear is the trigger that warns you something is wrong so listen to it and analyse the threat. If you are not confident, do not put your life at risk; work out a safer alternative. It is better to add time to your journey and arrive safely, than not to arrive at all. Similarly, don't walk through wooded areas at night, don't go down small isolated alleys in rough parts of a city and if you see a fight, or a gang of youths playing up, give them a wide berth.

Diet, Fitness and Self-defence

From any viewpoint diet, fitness and self-defence work together. Maintaining a good state of fitness will help protect your life, helping you cope with confrontational situations. Self-defence involves no magic formulas or archane art, there is no special technique that the SAS keep to themselves, there is only reality. If you are a middle-aged businessman, and are attacked by several thugs, your chances of beating them are slim. The reality is that they are likely to be fitter and quicker, while you, on the other hand, may have spent too long sitting behind a desk. Even if you are an accomplished self-defence expert, the odds are they will still beat you due to their numbers. The best option would be to run away or find help. To do this you must be fit and confident in your actions; the alternative is to lie down and take the punishment. Thus, maintaining a good state of fitness and well-being will help protect your life.

If you are overweight, you will not be able to react or respond quickly. If you are unfit, you will be unable to defend yourself for more than a few minutes

Any SAS soldier will tell you that the one weapon the regiment uses time and time again is speed and surprise. Your speed will come from good fitness training and practising various self-defence techniques until you are proficient. Surprise comes from having the confidence in yourself. Any attacker will normally pick on someone weaker or smaller than himself. You surprise him by facing up to him in a confident manner. You surprise him by preparing to fight. Best of all, you surprise him by getting in the first blow – one that makes him stop and think. Let's take a look at how fit you are and make a few suggestions for improvement.

YOUR LIFESTYLE

The old saying, 'your life is what you make it', is true. I have always believed that every individual can motivate themselves to whatever end they seek. Whatever your age, positive thinking is the key to cultivating a good lifestyle, and achieving a good state of physical fitness depends largely on your mental attitude. Determination is the main factor. For the average SAS soldier determination to get through selection and how far he gets in the Service will be directly related to his fitness. Those soldiers that pass selection achieve a state of fitness rarely found anywhere else in the world. Moreover, once in the regiment, the lifestyle of the SAS soldier continues to hone his body. In this way, his mind remains sharp, his body fit and healthy, and he has an assertive outlook on life. Such mental and physical well-being often brings with it the sense of being able to determine one's own destiny which contributes profoundly to personal confidence.

Analyse Your Lifestyle

Do you recognise your bad habits? Do you know how fit you are? The average SAS soldier does: he grades himself against his peers – you should do likewise. You have to be honest with yourself and define what state you are in now, and what state you would like to reach. This means examining every aspect of your home life, your work routine and your diet. Ask yourself some of these questions:

➤ Do you drink more than two pints of beer or the alcoholic equivalent each day?

➤ Do you have high blood pressure?

➤ Does your diet contain a regular supply of high-fat foods?

➤ Is your weight comparable with your height?

➤ Do you smoke?

➤ Do you exercise?

➤ Do you take drugs?

➤ Do you work in a dangerous environment?

➤ Do you live in a violent neighbourhood?

➤ Do you drive every day?

Lifestyle characteristics

If you aren't satisfied with your responses to these questions, do something about it. Plan to make a fresh start, taking it slowly, tackling one problem at a time. Choose either your diet, smoking, drinking, stress or exercise and set yourself a simple goal to start with. While exercising, make allowances for your age, sex and present state of health, all of which have an impact on what, and how much, you should do of it. The following is a general guide to typical lifestyles at different ages.

18 - 25 YEAR OLDS

These are the years where bad habits are formed. The average lifetime smoker will admit to having their first cigarette before the age of 14. By the time we reach 18 years of age most of us are hooked on social drinking. By contrast these years are when the body is at its peak of fitness. It is the time when you experiment with relationships and you start to understand what society is all about. It is also a dangerous age for men. We take risks, both at home, at work and during leisure, and the greatest killer is car accidents. Women in this age group are much more responsible in their social attitude, taking relationships more seriously and make the decision of a career more readily. Your social life, dancing and late nights will keep most people in this age group naturally fit. Chances of successfully defending yourself are 50/50.

26 - 36 YEAR OLDS

Men in this bracket start to catch up with women. They settle down into fatherhood and a steady work routine which protects the family interests, such as paying the mortgage and seeing to the families needs. The hyperactivity of youth is replaced with a daily work and home routine. For women it can be a dangerous time, particularly from the stresses of childbirth and family responsibilities. The body's fitness should still be maintained by the demands of looking after family and home. For most people the amount of smoking and drinking will have levelled off if not declined, as the money is needed to support the growing family. Chances of successfully defending yourself are 60/40 in your favour.

36 - 45 YEAR OLDS

For those that started smoking at an early age, this is their last chance to give up. If you do not quit by the time you are 45, there is little chance you will ever stop, and your chances of dying are greatly increased. At this stage most men mature and take life at a steadier pace and so lack of exercise increases the risk of heart disease. This is the time when you must realise that your body's calorie needs will start to decline. Alcohol intake is normally increased due to social status. Most women by this stage have had their last child. This is an important time to review lifestyles and fitness now needs constant attention. Chances of successfully defending yourself are 50/50.

46 -60 YEAR OLDS

From 46 onwards you really do need determination to snuff out bad habits. Heart disease is the main killer from now on, but if you take up steady exercise and do not try to be 21 again, then you can still improve your lifestyle and well-being. For women the menopause can cause both physical and mental problems. Long walks, gardening, and a careful diet will help maintain your fitness. Chances of successfully defending yourself are 30/70 against you.

60 YEARS PLUS

Live your life to the full. Eat a healthy diet and take daily exercise, don't just wait to die. Take time to talk to your partner, reminisce the finer points of your life together, plan to revisit old friends. Be an active grandparent, cultivate the young. Be happy and stay youthful. If you need help, don't be a victim of pride, we all get old. Chances of defending yourself at this stage 20/80 against you.

DEFINING YOUR AIM

We should all aim for good health and a long active life. Fitness must become a part of your life, and the younger you start, the better your body reacts. Being fit means you are less likely to suffer ill-health, in particular heart disease. Getting fit helps you enjoy life a lot more, you feel better, have more energy, and you look a whole lot better.

The advantages of exercise outweigh the risks of injury, but always listen to what your body is saying – if you feel pain, there is some reason for it. Watch where and how you exercise, and avoid doing too much. Exercise should be a part of your life, but don't let it take over your life.

We can all change if we really want to, and how quickly we change will depend on what obstacles we have to overcome. For most of us these obstacles are easy to identify – being overweight, unfit, smoking, too much alcohol, too much stress and so on – and before we can improve our fitness we must deal with these problems first.

GETTING RID OF BAD HABITS

We all have some bad habits, such as excessive eating, drinking, smoking, or even, in some cases, drug abuse and dependency. No matter how you argue the case for alcohol or soft drugs, neither one of these promote a healthy body or satisfactory lifestyle. What we must recognise in ourselves is that the habit is there. If, like many people, you have two or more bad habits then you have real problems. For example, if you drink and smoke excessively, the odds are you will die well before your time. The odd drink doesn't do

Get rid of any bad habits before you start getting fit

much harm, but a build-up of alcohol in the system over years will cause irreversible damage to the liver, eventually leading to death. Excess alcohol also has a deleterious effect on the heart, kidneys, brain and other organs. There is no doubt about it that alcohol in large amounts is a poison to the system. Another toxic habit is smoking. The tar contained in cigarettes is drawn into the lungs and will eventually cause many major health problems. Heart disease, lung cancer, throat and mouth cancer, and thrombosis are all associated with smoking and all have a high death rate. Neither do you need to be a smoker to end up with the same disorders: recent research has shown that those people who constantly breathe in other people's smoke are also at risk.

If you feel that you could have a problem, do something about it. Plan to make a fresh start but do it slowly and tackle one problem at a time, whether it is your diet, smoking, drugs, drinking, stress or lack of exercise, and set yourself a simple goal and start it NOW.

Alcohol

The relationship between alcohol and fitness is a balance, but quite simply the less you drink the fitter you are. If you drink too much alcohol then you need to bring your drinking under control. If you drink to excess, you will need to abstain altogether. If you drink socially, as most of us do, but feel you can control your drinking, you should still try to restrict the amount of alcohol you consume. You need only come up with a few reasonable excuses.

➤ I'm driving.
➤ I'm on prescribed drugs.
➤ I have a liver problem.
➤ I can't drink at lunchtime it makes me sleepy.
➤ Turn up late at parties and go home early.
➤ Drink mixers only and pretend they contain alcohol.
➤ Drink only every other day.
➤ Drink a glass of water between every alcoholic drink.

In the context of getting fit the only real option is abstinence. If you are only a social drinker then this will not be a problem. For those with a heavier consumption, it will do them the power of good to stop. Remember, alcohol is also fattening and the weight you lose when not drinking is a major bonus in itself.

Smoking

We all know that smoking is bad for our health, but if I were to say it interferes with physical fitness, I would be inundated with claims from very fit people who have always smoked. That said, I do urge those who

smoke to give it up – it kills more than 100,000 people in Britain alone. It is, however, a difficult habit to break and in the end it all comes down to willpower. Below is a list of suggestions that may help to bolster your resolve.

Stop Smoking

➤ Start a fitness aerobic programme.

➤ Tell everyone you are quitting – this puts pressure on you to do so.

➤ Find some activity that involves using your hands during period of relaxation.

➤ Remind yourself of the health benefits – longer and better life.

➤ Think of the financial benefits. Not just the cost of the cigarettes but your pension. You will have paid all those contributions and not lived to receive a pension.

➤ Don't think you're a failure if during some social function you are seduced into smoking several cigarettes – quit again next day.

Drugs

Many people admit to having taken drugs at one time

or another in their lives. For the majority of people this is partly due to peer pressure at such places like college, raves or nightclubs. However, for some, what might begin as a harmless, occasional stimulation for an evening's entertainment can soon become an addiction. However, giving up drugs is far harder than giving up alcohol and cigarettes. If you have a drug habit and really want to stop, then you need professional help. See your GP or go to one of the drug treatment centres.

Stress

Stress is emotional or physical strain and tension. Whether it becomes a problem depends largely on the level of stress, its duration and on our ability to contain and adapt to it. Major casuses of stress, known as 'stressors', include the death of a loved one, divorce, losing your job, taking on too much work (often combined with a poor working environment) and serious physical illness.

The warning signs of a person suffering from stress include persistent headaches (often severe), indigestion, sleeplessness, mood swings (perhaps sudden outbursts of anger), loss of concentration and poor appetite. There may also be a change in their habits, in particular they may drink and smoke more.

The most common stress-related illnesses (though stress may be only one factor) include digestive disorders (e.g. irritable bowel syndrome), stomach ulcers, blood pressure, eczema, effects on the immune system which can mean increased susceptibility to infections and mental problems such as panic attacks and even depression.

If you have a serious stress problem, then consult your doctor. However, whatever the severity, exercise and fitness will be of enormous help in reducing and combating stress.

Sleep

Sleeping is something we all do and need to do properly. It is an essential part of our lives especially when it comes to fitness and well-being. When we sleep the whole body relaxes totally. Many people suffer from a poor nights sleep, or an inadequate lack of hours requires to refresh the body. On average most of us sleep for around eight hours each night, however, it is quality rather than quantity which is important. Most people have experienced waking after a restful night feeling ready to take on the world. On the other hand we have all suffered from lack of sleep, where our night has been restless, short, or alcohol induced, and when we wake we feel more tired than when we went to sleep. Lack of a good night's sleep results in loss of concentration, poor work performance and as a detrimental effect on health. By far the largest single cause of sleeplessness is stress (see above) and general worrying.

One of the best ways to promote sleep is to have a good exercise routine, the fitter the body the better the sleep, no matter what the worries. Avoid taking naps during the day and establish a pre-sleep routine. Start winding down at least a couple of hours before your bedtime. Walk the dog, have a hot bath, watch the television or read a book – relax. It is best not to eat too late, or to drink too much alcohol just before going to bed. Milk contains trytophan, a substance which helps you sleep, so make a milky drink before bedtime. If you wake in the night, don't drink coffee or tea as these are stimulants and will keep you awake, try drinking tepid water instead.

Obesity

Obesity poses a serious health risk. There is only one real answer to the problem and that is to lose weight. Other than surgery the only way to achieve this is to consume fewer calories and steadily increase the amount of aerobic exercise taken.

The advantages of reversing the effects of obesity are numerous – a slimmer more attractive figure, a fitter and more agile body and a better lifestyle overall. What must be kept in mind is the time span over which any weight loss should occur. Because someone who is obese is unable to participate in strenuous exercise the

initial weight loss will be achieved through diet. This involves keeping strict control over calorie intake while maintaining the body's nutritional requirements. How much we need to lose and over what period of time can be discovered by simple mathematical equations (see the Body Mass Index on page 35).

By reducing your calorific intake (eating less) and increasing calorie burn by expending more energy (exercising), you should realistically expect a weight loss in the region of one or two pounds a week. It is not wise to try and lose weight by dieting alone, however, because the body will begin to think it is being starved and will compensate in other ways. It does this by slowing down its metabolic rate and as a result tends to conserve fat so that weight is lost very slowly. It is also a myth that diets should be a form of starvation. The body needs a minimum of around 1,500 calories a day to function properly, though some people may require more or less due to special circumstances. Also, it is nutritionally sensible that the calories should be spread out over all the major food groups.

Crash diets involving food regimes that work on a smaller calorie intake a day are best avoided as these tend not to produce lasting weight loss. They simply deplete body water and lean muscle tissue rather than body fat. The best diets take time and are usually combined with some form of exercise so that muscle tissue is maintained while fat is reduced. Aerobic exercise is the best type of exercise for reducing fat as the oxygen used is also necessary for the metabolization of fat into energy. Aerobic exercises include: jogging, swimming, walking, dancing, aerobics, cycling, stair-climbing, cross-country skiing, rowing and skipping. Whichever diet-and-exercise method you intend to use, it should be carried out in a safe and sensible fashion. See also Appendix Two: Eight-week – Two Stone Weight-loss Routine.

AUTHOR'S NOTE

➤ I once knew a woman aged around 35, who worked for an international drugs company. The first thing you noted was the clarity of her eyes, the second, her peach-like skin. I inquired as to how she achieved such a high state of beauty, her reply was simple: 'We are what we eat.' She virtually lived on fruit. She had been overweight for many years and decided to take up eating fruit whenever she was hungry.

ASSESSING YOUR CURRENT CONDITION

Let's assume that you have started to crack your old habits and now want to continue changing your lifestyle through diet and fitness. Before we go down that path we need to assess your present condition.

The best way to assess yourself is to stand naked in front of the mirror and turn around slowly. Next, to confirm your worst fears, step onto the bathroom scales and weigh yourself. Then work out your excess fat using the BMI method below and compare the results with the Height to Weight Chart below. (Note: If you have a small frame then deduct $4\frac{1}{2}$ lbs (2 kg) from the range, if you have a large frame, add $4\frac{1}{2}$ lbs (2 kg) to the range.)

WEIGHT TO HEIGHT CHART

Men		Women	
Height	**Av. Frame**	**Height**	**Av. Frame**
5' 4"	9-9.3 st	4' 11"	7.4-8.2 st
(1.62 m)	(56.5-62 kg)	(1.52 m)	(46-51.5 kg)
5' 5"	9.2-10 st	5' 1"	7.5-8.4 st
(1.65 m)	(57.5-63 kg)	(1.55 m)	(47-52.5 kg)
5' 6"	9.4-10.4 st	5' 2"	7.8-8.6 st
(1.68 m)	(59-65 kg)	(1.57 m)	(48.5-54 kg)
5' 7"	9.8-11 st	5' 3"	8-8.9 st
(1.70 m)	(61-69 kg)	(1.60 m)	(50-55.5 kg)
5' 8"	10-11 st	5' 4"	8.2-9.2 st
(1.72 m)	(62.5-69 kg)	(1.62 m)	(51.5-57 kg)
5' 9"	10.3-11.3 st	5' 5"	8.4-9.4 st
(1.75 m)	(64.5-71 kg)	(1.65 m)	(52.5-59 kg)
5' 10"	10.3-11.3 st	5' 6"	8.7-9.4 st
(1.78 m)	(66.5-72 kg)	(1.68 m)	(54.5-61 kg)
5' 11"	10.6-11.5 st	5' 7"	9-10.4 st
(1.80 m)	(68-75 kg)	(1.70 m)	(56.5-65 kg)
6' 0"	10.9-12 st	5' 8"	9.3-10.7 st

(1.83 m)	(70-77.5 kg)	(1.72 m)	(58-67 kg)
6' 1"	11.2-12.4 st	5' 9"	9.6-11 st
(1.85 m)	(72-79.5 kg)	(1.75 m)	(60-69 kg)
6' 2"	11.5-12.7 st	5' 10"	9.9-11.2 st
(1.88m)	(73.5-82 kg)	(1.78 m)	(62-70.5 kg)
6' 3"	12.1-13.4 st	5' 11"	10.1-11.5 st
(1.90m)	(76-84 kg)	(1.80 m)	(63.5-78 kg)
6' 4"	12.5-13.8 st	6' 0"	10.4-11.8 st
(1.93m)	(78-86.5 kg)	(1.83 m)	(65-73.5 kg)

BODY MASS INDEX (BMI)

The BMI is used to check your current weight not your physical fintess. BMI is defined as your weight in kilos divided by your height in metres squared. The recommended BMI in women is set between 18–23, while in men it is 21–26.

For example, for a woman who is 5 feet 6 inches tall and weighs 12 stone 5 lbs the calculation would be:

$$77.85 \text{ kilos} \div 2.72 \text{ m } (1.65 \times 1.65) = 28.62$$

(to convert lbs to kilos multiply by 0.45; to convert inches to metres multiply by 0.025)

The upper BMI limit in women is 23, which when subtracted from 28.62 leaves 5.62. This figure multiplied by the height squared, 2.72, equals 15.28, which is the number of kilos she is overweight.

The recommended weight loss per week is 2.25 lbs (1 kilo), therefore it will take some 15 weeks for her to achieve her goal.

Another more simple way of assessing weight is to grab the skin at the side of your waist between your fingers and thumb without pulling. Measure the overhang of skin and estimate the depth. If its more than a centimetre thick you are carrying excess fat. To estimate the amount ignore the first 2.5 cm (1 inch) then multiply every centimetre over this by 10 kg (22 lb). For example, if your skin pinch is 5 cm (2 inches) in total you will be roughly 25 kg (55 lb) overweight.

Do you weigh too much?

If you are within the BMI range and your weight and height fit in with the chart, give or take a few pounds, then you don't really need to lose weight. For those who are half a stone stone (3.1 kg) overweight first get a check-up from your doctor to make sure you are fit enough to start exercising. If you are more than a stone overweight, any exercise will carry the risk of serious injury as the added weight will impose extra strain on joints, and increase the already overworked organs such as your heart and lungs. Sudden, enforced exercise on an overweight body can lead to a heart attack. Consult your doctor and carry out the Weight-loss Routine first (see Appendix Two).

FITNESS TEST

Being of normal weight for your stature and height does not automatically mean you are fit, it simply means you are not carrying excess fat. Having established your weight, you now need to determine your present standard of fitness. This is a simple process whereby you monitor your heartbeat both at rest and during a set activity.

WARNING

Do not conduct the following fitness test if you have recently suffered from any illness, have heart problems, are taking prescribed medication or have been drinking heavily within the past 24 hours. Check the following questions and seek qualified medical advice if the answer to any is 'yes':

➤   Do you suffer from heart problems?

➤   Do you have high blood pressure?

➤   Do you suffer from chest pains?

➤   Do you suffer from dizziness or regular headaches?

➤   Do you have a medical condition that prevents exercise?

➤   Are you on medication?

➤   Are you 30 years or older and new to fitness?

➤   Are you seriously overweight?

Resting Heart Rate (RHR)

Sit quietly in a chair and relax for a full five minutes. Then check your pulse rate by placing two fingers on

the carotid artery in your neck or on the inner wrist. Count the total number of beats for 30 seconds then double the number – this is your resting heart rate. The average is around 75 beats to the minute. Slightly lower is excellent, but if your count is 85 or higher then you could have a problem.

Step Test

Find a step not less than 12 inches (30 cm) but not more than 16 inches (40 cm) high. Start stepping up and down at a non-stop, steady rate for 5 minutes.

Stop, sit in a resting position and take your pulse rate for 30 seconds, doubling the number to calculate for one minute.

The average should be around 140 beats. Lower is good but any higher and you are unfit.

Blood Pressure

Go to your doctor or practice nurse and get your blood pressure tested. Don't worry about being a pest as most surgeries encourage people to have a check-up. A normal person in their mid-thirties will have a blood pressure of around 120 over 80, but the doctor will indicate any risk if different.

How hard should we exercise?

That question is best answered by the individual and their weight and present level of physical fitness. Exercising means working the body harder than normal but if you exercise too much too soon the body will rebel, added to which it is very dangerous.

One of the best indicators of how your body is performing is the heartbeat. When resting the heart beats more slowly with a more relaxed rhythm, this is known as the resting heart rate (RHR). The harder we work the body the harder the heart works, but there is a limit, which is known as the maximum heart rate (MHR). As a form of guide you should exercise to around 70–75 per cent of your MHR, and this threshold is known as your training heart rate (THR).

To calculate your training heart rate you need to establish your RHR (see above). For the purpose of this calculation we take an average 25-year-old healthy person who is not on medication and has a RHR of 67. We must also determine the MHR, which is done by subtracting the age from the number 220, e.g. 220 - 25 = 195. This means that our individual could exercise their heart to where it reaches a maximum of 195 beats per minute.

Formula: 220 - age = maximum beats per minutes. In our example: 220 – 25 = 195.

The difference between out resting heart rate and our maximum heart rate is our heart rate reserve (HRR), which is calculated as follows: MHR - RHR = HRR.

195 - 67 = 128 beats per minute.

To find our training heart rate we simply calculate 70 per cent of the heart rate reserve and add it to our resting heart rate. Calculated as follows: 70% of HRR + RHR = THR.

0.70 x 128 + 67 = 156.6

As the body is exercised the heat rate increases, the muscles produce heat and the body warms. After several minutes and depending on the exercise (jogging) the body will settle and the increased heart rate will level off. After a period of 20 minutes or more you are free to check your heart rate, but make this as accurate as possible by counting the pulse beats for at least 30 seconds. If you find that your heart rate has jumped to more than your training heart rate, you should reduce exercise intensity, likewise if it below you should increase exercise intensity.

BASIC PRINCIPLES OF FITNESS AND EXERCISE

➤ You cannot exercise properly if you are grossly overweight.

➤ You cannot exercise for long if you cannot breathe efficiently.

➤ You cannot move freely without risk of injury if your body is inflexible.

➤ You cannot exercise effectively without strength and stamina.

People only get fit if they stick to the basic principles of exercise and diet.

You should find the right balance between diet and fitness.

You must exercise on a regular basis (ideally, three workouts per week up to a maximum of five).

Any physical exercise should be progressive (start off with less strenuous exercises and build the intensity and duration).

You will only become fitter when the workload of each exercise session exceeds that normally used by daily living demands.

STAGES OF ATTAINING FITNESS

Prolonged physical fitness increases the efficiency of the heart and lungs, which help to deliver oxygen and nutrients needed for muscular activity. Muscular strength is also improved, allowing muscle groups to be exerted for a longer period. The ability to move the joints or any group of joints with a greater degree of flexibility through a normal range of motions becomes easier while body fat is depleted.

There are several types of fitness, including aerobic, anaerobic, isometric and isokinetic. The range of exercises involved in fitness varies from walking (aerobic) through to using weight machines in a health club (isokinetic). Although all are beneficial, the aim of this book is to concentrate primarily on aerobic and muscular fitness through simple exercises such as walking, running and weightlifting.

Exercise Partners

For many of us, losing weight starts off as a very personal thing due mainly to our public declaration

that we are unfit or overweight. While you may wish to exercise alone, you will achieve far better results if you choose to exercise with one or more partners. The advantages are enormous, none more so than the maintenance of motivation. When you feel like giving up, your partner should impel you into continuing, and vice versa. Additionally, a common bond will develop that makes the routine more of a social pleasure than an individual endeavour. Some of the rewards of having good partners are:

➤ Shared motivation
➤ Good reliance on routine
➤ Stricter weight control
➤ Reduced exercise boredom
➤ Reduction in stress levels

FLEXIBILITY

Good flexibility can help you complete physical activities with greater efficiency and less risk of injury. The body can flex its muscles in a multitude of directions but there is no real test to determine the body's overall flexibility. Assessing the strain on

the hamstring and low-back areas is perhaps the best way of gauging flexibility. These areas are vulnerable to injury in most people, mainly due to loss of flexibility. A simple toe-touch test can be performed: stand with your legs straight and feet together and bend forward slowly at the waist – if you cannot touch your toes without vigorous bending then you need to improve your flexibility.

The best time to do stretching is during your warm-up and cool-down exercises (see opposite). The muscles should be stretched to full tension and a little beyond their normal capacity, causing strain but no pain. The range of stretching exercises varies from a gradual lengthening of the muscles as the body part moves around a joint to partner assisted stretching and muscle bouncing. For example, a slow rotation of the arms through their full range will help increase joint mobility and loosen-up the surrounding muscle, while jogging or walking on the spot for two minutes causes a steady raise in the heart rate, blood pressure and muscle temperature. Ideally, those stretching exercises used during a warm-up period should be held for around 10 seconds, while during the cool-down period the same exercise can be held for up to 20 seconds. The longer a stretch is held, the easier it is for the muscle to adapt to that length.

The type of flexibility exercise used should reflect on the muscle groups used during your main exercise period. If your main activity is a five-mile run then your flexibility exercises should include thigh and hamstring flexing. If you intend to do a session of muscular fitness, then your flexibility exercises should mimic those activities: for example, chest and abdominal flexing which helps prepare the neuromuscular pathways.

WARM-UP AND COOL-DOWN EXERCISES

Warm-up exercises increase body temperature. They also increase the range of joint movements and improve the speed of muscular contractions. The warm-up prepares the body in order that it will function throughout an energetic workout without injury.

By contrast many people do not understand the importance of cooling down after strenuous exercise. Cooling-down exercises bring the body back to its resting state in a measured way. To stop suddenly without any cool-down exercises will cause blood to

remain in the muscles thereby temporarily reducing the flow to the heart and brain. Feeling dizzy and faint directly after stopping any vigorous exercise are sure signs of this.

1   Start by deep breathing, fully exhale, then inhale slowly to a count of 10
2   Exhale to a count of 10
3   Repeat this three times

The purpose of this is to increase the amount of oxygen being delivered to the muscles, which in turn produce energy. Deep breathing will also help you relax and make your body go loose. Most warm-up exercises are simple rotation and have been around for many years. Rotation exercises are used to encourage joint lubrication and gently stretch the tendons, ligaments and muscles associated with a joint. Depending on how you feel, spend around 30 seconds to a minute on each exercise. Start off gently, working all your muscles through the full extent of their function, speed up slightly as your heart rate increases. Appendix One illustrates the more common stretching exercises.

AUTHOR'S NOTE

➤ One of the best ways to start off a warm-up session is by running on the spot. If you choose to listen to music while warming-up make sure that the tempo is not too quick; the idea is to relax.

Listening to music

Listening to music or an instructional tape is a great way of taking your mind off the monotony of your morning jog or exercise routine. However, it does present several dangers. First off,

46

running on a public highway while listening through a headset prevents you from hearing the traffic. Switch off and remove the headset wherever vehicles or moving machinery are present. Second, beware of the dangers of trying to stay in time with music or video exercises which have a fast beat.

Cardio-Respiratory Exercise (aerobic and anaerobic)

When we are threatened with danger we need more than anything to be able to breath for a sustained period without being exhausted. If you can maintain the air supply to the body you will have a much better chance against any assailant. You will be able to move quicker, run faster and for a longer duration; all this can be achieved through aerobic exercise. An aerobic exercise is one which is sustained steadily for a duration of time, typical examples are walking, running and swimming. These activities steadily increase the intake of air through the lungs while breathing. Anaerobic exercise, on the other hand, involves short bursts of activity, for example, tennis and football. These activities mainly use the oxygen which is stored in the muscles. In this book, for the most part, we will concentrate on aerobic fitness, which is aimed at increasing the heart rate. This increased heart rate, if sustained for 45 minutes or more, helps prompt the heart to grow more muscle, therefore next time we exercise we should find it marginally easier. A continuation of this process is known as 'physical fitness'.

The body's cardiovascular and respiratory systems function together, especially during exercise or work, to ensure that adequate oxygen is supplied to the working muscles to produce energy for muscular contraction. When muscle activity is sustained they become tired, and the point at which this tiredness occurs is relative to the oxygen circulating in the system. A high level of cardio-respiratory fitness permits continuous physical activity without a decline in performance and allows for rapid recovery following fatiguing physical activity.

AUTHOR'S NOTE

➤ Aerobic exercise ensures that a greater amount of air passes through the lungs. This also increases the pumping action of the heart, so improving the efficiency with which the oxygenated blood is circulated to the working muscle and waste products are removed from the system.

SAS AEROBIC FITNESS DEFINITIONS

Different exercises, varying stages of fitness and terrain all demand modification in the amount of effort put into the overall workout. For example, some exercises which involve walking or running over rough terrain will physically be more demanding than doing the same exercise on a flat road. Simple aerobic exercise raises your heart rate, increases oxygen intake and improves blood flow. It will tone muscle and reduce body fat. However, you must exercise to suit your body weight; the heavier you are the slower you should perform. After a while, the more weight you lose the faster you can go. The reason for this is simply to avoid injury. These differentials are best described as follows:

Pace

➤ Walking pace should average 18 minutes per mile.

➤ Jogging pace should be around 12–15 minutes per mile.

➤ Slow Running 10 minutes per mile.

➤ Normal Running 8 minutes per mile.

➤ Short fast run 5–6 minutes per mile.

Normal Rate

Run at the same pace making sure you can maintain a steady rhythm to your breathing. This should be about 70–80 per cent of best-effort pace.

Best Effort

Best effort means just that, giving it 100 per cent plus.

Always make sure that you have warmed up properly before starting out on a best-effort run, and that you cool down after. As with all the exercise tasks, start off at a good but controllable pace, speed up and then push yourself to the limit for the final third.

Hill Repetitions

Find a steep slope, which is at least 200 metres long with an incline of around 30 degrees or more. It should take no more than a minute to sprint to the top. Sprint up the hill, then jog down to recover. Hill reps are designed to build your leg power and lung capacity. One hill rep is classified as 'sprint up, jog down'. Take short sharp steps and lean into the hill, relax as you jog down.

Jogging

Jogging is little more than fast walking and the secret of jogging is duration, not speed. Time on your feet is what's important. Start your jogging programme only after two weeks of walking, especially if you are new to fitness. Once you start jogging, concentrate on a pace that suits you. Jog with a heel first action, letting the toes claw into the pace and push off with the ball of your foot. Jog within your breathing capabilities, that is, run at a pace where you can hold a normal conversation.

Running

It may sound silly but many people have forgotten or don't know how to run properly. The first thing to do is make sure your footwear is suited to the terrain you

will be covering – blisters can be extremely painful. Run with your body in an upright relaxed posture and let your arms adopt a natural swinging motion between your waist and chest. Run lightly making sure that your footstrike hits the ground with rhythmic timing. Shorten your step on the incline and extend it slightly on the decline. If your route takes you over uneven ground, be careful to avoid stepping on loose or protruding objects. Don't run too fast – you should be able to talk.

The terrain over which you run should also be considered. There is no need to take a dangerous route over rocky or marshy ground. Choose your route for its even pathways, its scenic beauty and its ease of access. If the route has very steep inclines then vary your pace accordingly.

Press-ups

Press-ups could be called the mainstay of fitness – certainly as far as most armed services are concerned. Again, like all exercises, press-ups can be easy or hard but the important thing is to do them correctly.

1 Lay face down, arms bent in the frog position, palms flat on the ground directly under the shoulders, body flush to the floor, legs and feet together.

2 Raise your head, look forward and gently ease a rigid body off the floor using your arms. The position is correct when both the arms and body are straight.

3 Relax in a controlled attitude by bending your arms back to the frog position.

The single most common mistake that is made by beginners is allowing the stomach and hips to sag. Although this will have the effect of making the exercise easier, it also removes 90 per cent of the benefit which defeats the whole object and makes the exercise pointless. Press-ups can be varied in a number of ways. For example, the feet can be raised on a step or low chair, or the hands can be placed closer together under the upper chest, both of which require a lot more effort.

You can do press-ups almost anywhere, all you need is a space that is as long as your body. Also, for such a simple exercise that requires no equipment, they work a whole range of body muscles from the neck down to the toes. If you are fairly new to exercise, start with just 10 press-ups and repeat as you feel able. When you feel fit enough increase the number to four bouts of 25 spread over your training session.

Skipping

Skipping is a low risk, aerobic exercise that can be done by almost anyone, no matter what their weight or lack of fitness. It can be made as hard or easy as it needs to be. Athletes and performers of all kinds, from boxers to ballerinas, use skipping as part of their work-outs. This is because it provides hard exercise but without the risk of serious injury. Unlike jogging or running, skipping is regarded as a low-impact exercise.

The other advantage is that it only requires a skipping rope and a flat surface – no fancy equipment or expensive gym membership. The best type of rope to buy is a professional leather rope, which are inexpensive, are of the right weight and long-lasting. Even those who are as yet unable to jog or go on long walks due to breathing difficulty will still be able to participate gently in this exercise.

Start off slowly and aim to jump just high enough to clear the rope as it swings under your feet. Try and keep a constant rhythm without faltering for at least a minute then have a little rest. Once you have your breath back, skip again for another minute. Persistence will help to build up the lung capacity and muscles, and you will soon be able to skip for longer and longer. Once you are really proficient, try taking the knees higher as well.

Skip with both feet together or by taking running steps. Beginners tend to find it easier to run lightly on the balls of their feet, but once you get faster, jumping with both feet together on the spot will most probably be the preferred option. The rope itself should be swung by rotating the forearm and the wrist only, and making sure that the rope just skims the ground. At first many people leave the rope too slack, which then bounces on the floor and becomes tangled with the feet. Make sure that your elbows are tucked firmly into your waist and that you stand

straight, with your shoulders back and your head up. Once you have reached the stage where you feel you have settled into a steady routine and speed, you should then attempt to do four sessions of between two and three minutes within an hour. This will not only greatly improve your lung capacity but it will also build up the muscles in your calves and lower legs – which will be a great benefit when you need to run from an assailant.

Swimming

Apart from running over the hills every SAS soldier entering the Regiment must pass a basic swimming test. In the beginning this test is normally swimming fully clothed in the local baths, but later the annual test is often done by swimming a mile in the sea. For those who cannot swim there is usually a crash course. If you cannot swim, you are advised to go to your local swimming pool and enrol for a course. It is normally not expensive, and the students are put into groups according to age. The basics of swimming can be learnt in just a few lessons and improved at your leisure.

However, to get any real fitness benefit from swimming you need to swim relatively fast for at least half an hour at each session. While simply swimming up and down may feel good it will do little to improve your fitness. You should give yourself a time limit, for example, 30 minutes, and see how many lengths of the pool you can achieve in that time.
As with cycling, swimming has several advantages. It is possible to do it while suffering from some form of injury as the water supports the body's weight. Swimming is also excellent for asthma sufferers as it does not provoke exercise-induced asthma.

Cycling

Cycling is an excellent alternative to running. Indeed, you can cycle when suffering from leg strains caused by running. The distance covered on a bike is roughly five times that of running, although both are achieved with the equivalent energy burn.

Choose where you cycle with care. Cycling in traffic is dangerous and unpleasant, while mountain biking is very prone to accidents. A hard-surface route fairly free of traffic is ideal. You must always wear a cycling helmet. If you intend to do long distances on a racing bike, padded shorts are essential, also a water-bottle.

As with running, it is duration that is important. If you are not used to cycling, take it easy to start with, and make sure the bike is adjusted to suit your body and pedal stride. Begin with short (five-mile) routes and build up the distance slowly. This will give the muscle groups around the upper thigh and buttock time to become active. Get used to anticipating the inclines and declines ahead of you and so adjust your gearing.

MUSCLE STRENGTH AND STAMINA

If you are forced to fight you will need both muscle strength and stamina in addition to cardio-respiratory fitness. The ability to deliver a swift hard blow with accuracy is a major asset in any confrontation. Muscular strength is the greatest amount of force a muscle or muscle group can exert in a single effort. Muscular endurance is the ability of a muscle or muscle group to do repeated contractions against a less-than-maximum resistance for a given time. Although muscular endurance and strength are separate fitness components, they are closely related. Progressively working against resistance will produce gains in both of these components. There are two methods by which this can be achieved:

➤ Isometric contraction, which produces contraction but no movement, for example, when pushing against an immovable object. Force is produced with no change in the angle of the joint.

➤ Isotonic contraction, which causes a joint to move through a range of motion against a constant resistance. Examples of this are push-ups, sit-ups and the lifting of weights.

For a muscle to increase in strength the workload to which it is subjected during exercise must be increased beyond what it normally encounters; this is

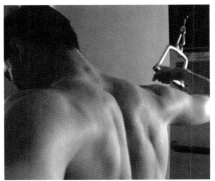

known as muscle overload. Muscles acclimatize to increased workloads by becoming larger and stronger and by developing greater endurance. This is accomplished by using an exercise weight which lets you do 8 to 12 repetitions of a particular exercise correctly before the muscle becomes fatigued. Finding the correct weight for each exercise is a matter of trial and error and will vary from individual to individual. In principle if you cannot carry out three repetitions of a particular exercise the weight is too heavy and should be reduced. On the other hand, if you are able to carry out 20 repetitions without muscle fatigue, then the weight is too light. Initially, you should choose a weight resistance that lets you do around 12 repetitions of a given exercise.

A sustained training program using the correct weight will significantly improve muscle endurance and strength. The key to overloading a muscle is to make that muscle exercise harder than it normally does. An overload may be achieved by any of the following methods:

➤ Increasing the weight.
➤ Increasing the number of repetitions.
➤ Increasing the number of sets.
➤ Decreasing the rest time between sets.
➤ Speed of exercise movement.

As with all forms of exercise results depend on the individual, but in principle muscle fitness can only be achieved by progressively increasing the weight, number of repetitions and number of repetition sets. When you can correctly do the upper limit of repetitions for the set without reaching muscle failure, it is time to increase the resistance. For most people this upper limit should be 12 repetitions.

GYM vs. HOME EQUIPMENT

There is some debate about where you should exercise, whether in a gym or in your own home. At a gym you are usually supervised and monitored by professional staff, which is important if you are new to exercise or have no exercise partner. On the other hand there is the cost both in time and money, enrolment is usually for a minimum of six months and few people have a gym on their doorstep. For many there is also an ambarrassment factor and of being intimidated.

If you feel you are not yet ready to face the gym then you could consider working out at home. While this saves time and allows you to exercise at differing periods throughout the day it also requires a lot more discipline. Most people go off and buy several items of equipment convinced that they will provide them with the body they desire. In reality most of the equipment gathers dust in the garage or spare room. So if you intend to exercise at home, think it through first before buying any expensive equipment.

Multi-exercise Station

Multi-exercise stations, or variable resistance weight machines, are now available in most good gymnasiums. These are a pieces of equipment designed to do a number of different exercises. At the top end of the scale a good quality multi-exercise station will put the whole body through a series of exercises designed to work all the muscle groups. The added advantage of theses machines is their ability to vary the resistance of each exercise, putting the muscle under tolerable but not excessive tension during the tension and relaxation phase of each exercise. Another big advantage of a multi-exercise station is its safety over the more traditional 'free' weights, which you could become trapped under. Weight machines are extremely safe as the bulk of exercises are controlled via a pulley system that has a preset stop position, which allows individuals to train at home or unsupervised. A further benefit of working out on a weight machine is that most of your routine can be done in the same place. Additionally, such machines can be adjusted to compensate for the beginner through to the fittest person by moving a pin to vary the resistance.

Where time is a factor it may be worthwhile considering the purchase of weights or a weight machine for use at home. When compared to the cost of enrolling in a fitness club for a year they can be also very cost effective, added to which you can exercise when convenient and save time travelling to your gym. Most larger supermarkets now carry a good range of fitness and exercise equipment. Whether you choose to exercise in the home or in a gym you should seek advice on their usage and exercise with caution and supervision until you become proficient. For a detailed muscle strength and stamina programme see Appedndices Three and Four.

AUTHOR'S NOTE

➤ Some years ago, some friends brought me a punch-bag and a set of sparring gloves for my birthday. They had purchased the gift more as a joke rather than for me to use; but use them I did. I stuffed the bag with an old duvet and hung it from my garage. I found it wonderful for overall fitness training. It improved my flexibility, and built muscle power both which helped improve my self-defence techniques. More than anything it improved my breathing, as breathing can be improved by regular exercise. Now I understand how boxers can stay on their feet for so long after receiving so much punishment. I can honestly say there is no better way of staying fit, controlling your breathing, and practising your self-defence skills than punching the hell out of a bag for half an hour.

(contd)

➤ Warm up with five minutes skipping.

➤ Ten minutes shadow boxing. Take it easy, pace yourself.

➤ Five minutes skipping.

➤ Five minutes fast boxing.

➤ Five minutes fast skipping, on your toes.

➤ Always relax for a few minutes at the end of your fitness routine.

The Law

SELF-DEFENCE, JUSTIFICATION, AND PROVOCATION

A brief summary of the legal view of self-defence, justification and provocation is as follows:

➤ Anyone is entitled to use reasonable force to defend themselves, their property, or another person. In addition, a person may use such force as is reasonable in the circumstances in the prevention of crime.

➤ Where a defendant puts forward a justification for the infliction of violence, such as self-defence, provocation or resistance to violence, the onus is on the prosecution to disprove these matters if a verdict of guilty is to be justified.

➤ The degree of force permissible depends on whether the defendant's actions were reasonable in the circumstances. When the issue of self-defence is raised, it is an important consideration that the accused should have demonstrated by his actions that he did not want to fight. It has been said that a person must have shown that he was prepared to temporise and disengage and perhaps make some physical withdrawal but it was subsequently made clear that a failure to retreat is only an element in the considerations upon which the reasonableness of an accuser's conduct is to be judged; in some circumstances a person might act in self-defence and have a good defence without temporising, disengaging or withdrawing.

➤ However, the test of reasonableness is not entirely objective and the state of mind of the accused should not be overlooked completely.

➤ A breach of the peace can only be justified when used to prevent a breach of the peace, although the circumstances of a provocation may be taken into consideration in awarding the punishment. Provocation does not alter the nature of the defence, but it is allowed for in the sentence.

Common sense in self-defence

Put more simply, you may use only 'reasonable force' to defend yourself or others from an attack. What you see as reasonable will depend entirely on the situation and its progress. For example, if you really believe that you or someone else is about to be murdered, then you can use any appropriate method to stop the assault. However, this does not give you free licence to murder the assailant. Likewise if you have used a metal bar to beat the assailant, to the point where there is no further risk from him, you are breaking the law if you continue your attack. In essence, you must only do the minimum that is required to stop or avoid further injury. If, in the cold light of day, the assailant that originally picked on you ends up in hospital with a broken skull, the courts may well find that your actions were excessive. However, the courts do recognise that

> ... a person defending himself cannot weigh to a nicety the exact measure of his necessary defensive action. If... in a moment of unexpected anguish a person had only done what he honestly and instinctively thought was necessary that would be most potent evidence that only reasonable defensive action had been taken.

Additionally, the law will have expected you to extract yourself from any impending violence, not confront it (but does accept that this is not always possible). Finally, remember, you are not allowed to go about the street armed with any article that is intended for violence.

Do Not Carry Weapons

If you are attacked and even injured, and you are carrying a weapon you will be charged; self-defence using an article that is outside the law, is no excuse. Guns, knives, clubs and knuckle dusters are all illegal. Stanley knives and other DIY tools fall into a very grey area, as do baseball bats, and garden tools. Everyday items such as umbrellas, keys, a torch (at night), hairsprays and magazines are permissible, but only used with reasonable force. (See Using Everyday Items as Weapons on p.90).

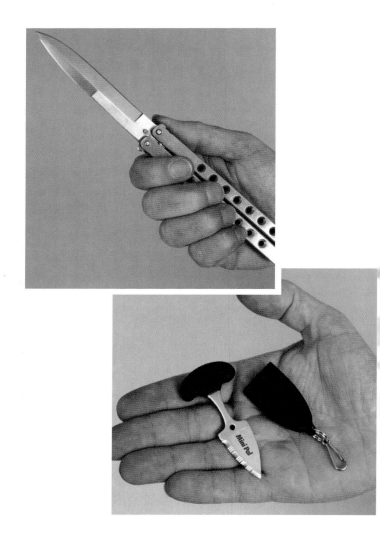

Do not consider carrying an illegal weapon such as these, a butterfly knife (top) and a keyring knife (bottom)

SAS ACTION

➤ There was once an SAS soldier who was on a secret training operation in Hong Kong. He went out on the town one night with a member of the Hong Kong police force. After a few drinks both men found themselves embroiled in a fight with some local Chinese. While the policeman decided to make a run for it the SAS solider stood his ground, dropping several of his assailants with little or no trouble. Then the local police arrived to break up the brawl, which is when they found the knuckle-duster in the SAS man's hand. He was arrested. Early next morning he stood in front of a judge and was offered a week in jail or ten lashes of the cane after which he would be released. To preserve his anonymity he opted for the lashes, thinking that with his punishment over he could return to work with his team commander none the wiser. The lashes where so severe that he was hospitalised for several weeks, after which he was dismissed from the SAS (although he did return to the the Regiment some years later).

Items which are purposely designed to be weapons are mostly illegal. Most of them will do more damage than is necessary for you to disengage yourself from a potentially dangerous situation. Delivering a blow with a cosh will cause terrible damage – hit someone in the right place and you could be held up for murder. Concealed blades may make you feel confident but in reality they are little more than ornamental, but if the police discover one on you, you could end up in jail.

Never carry a gun, even a fake one. If you carry a gun that fires some form of projectile strong enough to deter a mugger, you still run the risk of being shot by the police. Guns ring alarm bells with the police authorities, and anyone thought to be carrying a gun will be confronted by armed police.

Carrying Weapons Abroad

Don't be tempted to conceal weapons in your baggage or on your person, airport security is extremely efficient and the likelihood of getting caught is very high. Even if you manage to sneak something through an airport, being found with an offensive weapon in a foreign country will almost certainly land you in very hot water. You may think that in countries where violence is high that the odd can of spray irritant, or a knuckle-duster would be seen as a normal precaution – not so. Being arrested for fighting is one thing, having an offensive weapon in your possession is another.

You may also be tempted to purchase so-called self-defence weapons which are on full view in many foreign shops. For example, in Spain it is just a matter of walking into the appropriate shop where you can buy any number of items, coshes, butterfly blades, concealed blades, knuckle-dusters and guns (though these guns are not real, in as much as they work on compressed air, but they will still inflict serious damage).

Threats to kill

In many trivial situations, people have often verbally threatened to kill another person. If this involves an ongoing feud, and a serious attack is made on that person, the threat to kill becomes a matter of law, so be careful what you say:

A person who without lawful excuse makes to another a threat, intending that the other would fear it would be carried out, to kill that other or third person shall be guilty of an offence and liable on conviction on indictment to imprisonment of a term not exceeding ten years.

A lawful excuse can exist if a threat to kill is made for the prevention or for self-defence, providing that it is reasonable in the circumstances to make such a threat; the onus is on the prosecution to prove that there was no lawful excuse for making the threat.

INVOLVEMENTS WITH THE POLICE

From birth to death, laws govern our lives. They are there to protect both the individual and the society –

we must obey the law and work within it. No matter what our personal opinion of the police, they are there to uphold the law. We are lucky in Britain to possess a police force that is well disciplined and fair. If you have been involved in a confrontation, never hinder the police: they are there to help.

When you are involved in any public conflict to which the police are called, the following advice should be adhered to:

➤ Stay calm.

➤ Do not get dragged into an argument.

➤ Think about what you say, and say very little.

➤ Treat the police with respect, and do exactly what they say.

➤ Take into consideration that the police too are human, and sometimes the situation as they see it may initially place you in a bad light, particularly if you have used some object or article to defend yourself. If they make an error in judgement, co-operate until you have the opportunity to explain yourself.

If you feel that you are not being treated in a lawful manner, take the police officer's number and report the incident at the station. All police officers, whether in uniform or civilian clothes, should identify themselves to you. If you are ever unsure, telephone their station for confirmation.

The witness statement

If you are involved in an incident where an unlawful act has taken place, being an eyewitness and giving an accurate witness statement is very important.

Even if you are directly involved in the incident, always try to construct a clear mental picture of the scene, talking it through to yourself.

RECORDING AN INCIDENT

➤ What is actually happening as you see it?

➤ How did the incident start?

➤ What is the sex of those involved?

➤ What is the age of those involved?

➤ Get a good description – complexion or skin colour, hair colour and style, shape of the face, with any clear distinguishing marks.

➤ What is each person is wearing?

➤ Who is holding, or using any weapon or implement?

➤ If you are not directly involved, carefully note the action of each person.

➤ What type of vehicle is involved: is it a car or motorbike, etc? How old is the vehicle, and what condition is it in?

(contd)

➤ What is the vehicle's registration, colour and make?

➤ Get details of all occupants.

➤ In what direction did the vehicle go?

The Basics of Self-defence

Trouble and conflict normally start for one of two reasons. First, you have become involved in an argument, be it your own or someone else's. Secondly, another person, or a number of people, have premeditated an attack on you. In the first instance, you should, with logical discussion, be able to extract yourself without harm, even if this means losing the argument. A fight will only start when neither side, due to ego, pride and plain stubbornness, will back down far enough to defuse the situation. These confrontations rarely lead to serious injury and common sense coupled with respect should stop things going too far. It is when an argument starts and one of the participants is intoxicated that the situation is difficult to stop.

Someone who is totally drunk will be more mouth than action, as the alcohol will slow him down and disorientate his movements. The danger lies in the opponent who has drunk sufficiently to bolster his Dutch courage and affect his reasoning ability, but not enough physically to hamper him. If you try to extract yourself, he may see this as a sign of weakness

and make a sudden rush at you. At this point you will be forced to defend yourself.

A premeditated attack is normally carried out through lack of respect, immaturity, excitement, excess alcohol, or more likely, for profitable gain. Many premeditated attacks will leave the victim with serious damage or injury, and in the most extreme cases, dead. The secret of avoiding any such attack on your person is awareness and preparation. Awareness should take away the element of surprise from your assailant, and preparation will help you defend yourself.

In any confrontational situation, stay calm and stay ready. Never allow your reasonable behaviour to be mistaken for weakness. Defuse the situation by looking confident, while seeking avenues of escape. Remember, if your opponent has been drinking heavily, he will not be able to run very far before he becomes short of breath. If a fight looks imminent, get your blows in first, do it quickly and with all the aggression you can muster.

BALANCE

Martial arts, no matter what form they take, all depend on one single factor: balance. We need to acquire the skill necessary to overcome any antagonist.

To this end, there is one outstanding principle: Without body balance there is no strength

Establishing your balance

To utilise our body strength and exert that strength against any antagonist, we must have balance. For if your body is not properly poised, and thus unbalanced, any struggle between two unarmed people will rely on pure muscular exertions and the stronger person will win.

In order to win against a stronger person, you must adopt a positive mental attitude, which will settle you into a pre-trained 'on guard' stance. This will automatically put your body into a well-balanced position from which you can use your body strength to its full advantage. The 'on guard' stance is discussed below.

Unbalancing your assailant

Your other main aim is to unbalance your assailant. He can be pushed backwards, pulled forwards, and moved to either side but the construction of the hip and knee joints enable him to regain his balance by simply stepping in the same direction as his body is moving.

However, if he is pulled or pushed diagonally, a slight loss of balance occurs immediately, the reason being that the knee joint is not hinged in the corner-ways direction. The leg becomes stiff at once, and causes the assailant to step across with his other foot in order to retain his upright posture. To stop any attack and press home your advantage, you must get your assailant into this unbalanced position, while maintaining your own balanced stance.

THE 'ON GUARD' POSITION

The 'on guard' position, shown opposite, is the first combat move any new SAS recruit is taught during his self-defence lessons. It is not complicated and means standing and moving like a boxer.

To adopt the on-guard position:

➤ Stand facing your opponent.

➤ Part your feet until they are about the width of your shoulders.

➤ Favour one leg slightly forward, and bend your knees.

➤ Keeping your elbows tucked in, raise your hands to protect your face and neck.

It is best to practice this move in front of a large mirror – stand relaxed, then with a slight jump, go into the 'on guard' position. Do not stiffen, try to feel comfortable. Tell your body it is a spring at rest.

Movements from the on-guard position

First try using your hands: throw out your favoured hand in a blocking motion while at the same time automatically placing the other hand in front of your lower face. This will protect your mouth and nose but will not obscure your vision.

Next, imagine that someone is about to punch you in the stomach. Keep your stance, elbows in tight and twist your shoulders from the waist, moving round to meet the blow. You will find that this puts the muscle of your forearm in a protective position, without having to move your feet or upsetting your balance. To practise your balance, move about the floor, first sliding one foot back and drawing the other one after it quickly until, no matter how you move, you can always stop instantly in balance, not by shuffling your feet into position, but with clean-cut, precise movements.

When you have to move, try to flow. Do not lift your feet, unless you intend to kick. Do not cross your legs or you will lose your stance. Move in the opposite direction of any attack. Practice your 'on guard' position, and movements from this position, with a partner, or use a punch bag.

PROTECTING YOUR BODY

The human body is well adapted to taking punishment, and will survive terrible assault. During an assault, we must protect the most vulnerable parts of our bodies. Conversely, knowing the most vulnerable body parts is useful when you are forced to fend off an attacker.

Vulnerable part of the body

The body has many vulnerable areas which can make suitable targets in your defence. The diagram opposite shows the main points at which your strikes should be directed.

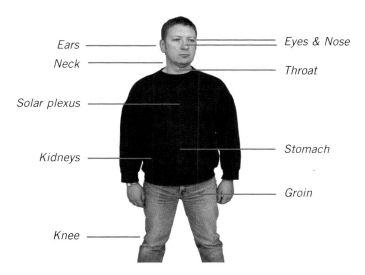

Ears — Eyes & Nose

Neck — Throat

Solar plexus —

Stomach

Kidneys — Groin

Knee —

Eyes

Without our eyes we are fairly helpless. Damage to an attacker's eyes, causing temporary or even permanent loss of vision, will allow you to escape. Note: the justification for blinding an attacker must be a last resort, e.g. when your life is in grave danger, or to prevent a serious attack such as rape.

Ears

Ears are a good target to attack, offering themselves readily available for you to bite. Sinking your teeth into someone's ear lobe will have the desired effect if you are being attacked. A long, sharp fingernail will also produce a large amount of pain. Clapping your open palms over both your attacker's ears will produce a rather nasty numbing sensation in the head, and has been known to cause unconsciousness.

Nose

Like the ears, the nose protrudes and therefore offers a good target to bite or strike with your fist. Use as much force as is necessary to make your attacker break off the attack. Any upward blow will make the attacker lift his head and offer his throat for punishment. As with the ears, a sharp fingernail pushed up the nostril will be very painful.

Neck and throat

The neck and throat area is a very vulnerable target, as it contains most of the life-support vessels that keep us alive. Both main blood vessels that supply the brain are located close to the skin surface

on either side of the neck. Damage to either blood vessel can result in death. The airway in the throat is also easy to damage, and a simple blow will incapacitate your attacker allowing you time to escape. A single sharp blow to the back of the neck can also cause a temporary black-out.

Stomach and solar plexus

A heart punch, aimed at the point on the chest where the ribs start to separate, will have a devastating effect on any attacker. The same blow delivered with force to the stomach will literally knock the wind out of a person.

Testicles

Although a good kick or blow to the groin will hurt a woman, it will cause triple the pain to a man. It is also possible to grab and twist a man's testicles. While this procedure may seem repellent, it will produce the most dramatic effect in your attacker.

Lower legs

A backward blow against either knee joint is guaranteed to stop any attacker chasing after you. The legs are also a good area to kick when you are being held in a bear hug, or gripped from behind. Stamping down hard on the attacker's toes will also have the desired effect.

THE BODY'S WEAPONS

In a situation where no other weapons are available, you must defend yourself with your body's weapons. Select which is appropriate to the situation and when you decide to strike, move with all the speed and aggression you can muster. Remember: adopt your 'on guard' position and think about your actions.

The single devastating blow

If you have managed to unbalance your assailant, and in doing so left him open to your assault, try the instant follow-up. Your first defence will have the effect of making your assailant think twice – take advantage of this and follow through with one good blow. Assess his position, calculate his next action, and move before he can recover.

The secrets of success

Done properly, the 'devastating blow' will get you out of most situations. The following are tips to help you develop your technique;

➤ Recognise the precise moment when you should strike one swift, sharp and accurate blow, driven home when your assailant is unbalanced. This movement can be practised without an opponent – a punch bag will prove invaluable.

➤ Learn to develop a good knockout punch. It may not work on everyone, but it will make any attacker think. Most street fighting will only last for a few seconds, so getting one good blow in may make your attacker break off the contact and look for easier pickings. You do not need great strength to deliver a good punch – it is a matter of manoeuvrability, speed and timing.

➤ Develop a short sharp jab: using a tight fist, rotate your arm from the shoulder first before extending the elbow. Aim to deliver the maximum force at some point beyond your actual point of contact. Do not swing your blow; keep it short, sharp and hard.

DELIVERING THE BLOW

➤ If your opponent is down on the ground, use your feet: kick him in the kneecap or stamp down on his testicles. Your aim should be to incapacitate your assailant and stop him chasing after you.

➤ If he is still standing and you have your back slightly towards him, you may be perfectly placed to deal him a damaging blow to the stomach with your elbow.

➤ If he is facing you, and his face is not too far

away, strike him at the side of the neck with the little finger edge of your hand. Use a sharp motion, hand held rigidly, and the arm bent at the elbow to form a right-angle. In this way you have an arm and hand that can be swept round like a scythe: a striking weapon some 18 inches in length. The same movement can be aimed at the temple, but this time striking with the back of a balled fist.

Screaming

The power of your voice is often overlooked as a weapon in your arsenal. At its simplest, sceaming at your attacker may surprise or un-nerve him (and may also draw attention to your situation, bringing help). However, coupled to your attack, screaming adds extra impetus to a strike, focusing all your energy. This is a particularly useful weapon for women to use in threatening situations.

Punch

When someone is attacked, it is an instinctive response for them to strike back with a punch. **Try to avoid this technique.** If your hand hits a hard target, such as your attacker's head, it is likely you will break bones in your knuckles or fingers, leaving

you injured and vulnerable. If you do punch your assailant, make sure you aim for a soft target, such as the stomach. However, open hand techniques such as palm strikes and strikes with the edge of the hand are more effective and safer for you. If you must punch, learn how to do it properly. If you make a fist

incorrectly, you risk hurting yourself more than your assailant. To make a correct fist, curl your fingers into your palm and lock your thumb over them. Never curl the fingers over the thumb or let your little finger stick out. When punching, the wrist must be locked and the line of the forearm should follow straight to the knuckles. Don't draw back your arm to punch – it announces your intentions and allows any strike to be blocked. The power in a punch should come from the legs and the twisting effect of the waist.

Open palm

Slapping the open palms simultaneously against the ears, either from the back or from the front will cause damage to your assailant. Using a chopping motion against

the side and rear of the neck is also very effective. If your assailant is young or elderly, consider a vigorous slap across the face.

Heel of the hand

The chin jab is delivered with the heel of the hand, putting the full force of your body weight behind the punch. When attacking from the front, spread the fingers and go for the eyes. If attacking from the rear, strike the back of the neck just below the hair line for a very effective punch. As the head snaps forward, use your fingers to grab the hair and snap it back quickly. You are less likely to injure your hand using the heel of the hand.

Edge of the hand

The edge-of-the-hand blows are executed by using the outer edge of the hand, i.e. little-finger side. Keep your fingers straight with your thumb extended. Your arm

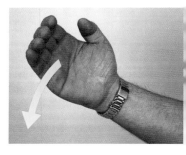

should always be bent, never straight, when delivering this blow. Use a chopping action from your elbow and have your body weight behind it. Cut downwards, or across, using either hand, moving your hand outwards with your palm always facing down.

Elbow

 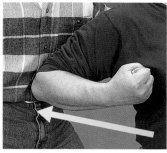

A great weapon when you are side-on or have your back to the assailant. Jabbing the elbow into your assailant's stomach will almost certainly drop him to the floor. If you have been knocked to the ground, try elbowing up into the testicles. Any well-connected blow from your elbow will give you time to break contact and run.

Knee

Although it is one of the body's more powerful weapons, it is limited by its movement, restricting it to the lower part of the body. However, its battering-ram effect can cause severe damage when driven into the testicles or aimed at the outer thigh, causing a dead-leg.

Foot

A hard kick is as good as any fist punch, and can be used just as readily. Keep your kicks below waist height, unless you have had some special training. Remember, however, the moment you lift your foot from the floor, you become

unbalanced. Although there are a few exceptions, a kick with your boot should be done sideways. By doing so, you will be putting more force behind the blow and you will, if needed, be able to reach farther.

Heel

If grabbed from behind, your heel is an excellent weapon. Drive it down the instep of your assailant or stamp continually on his foot. Another effective way to use the heel is to kick at the ankle bones.

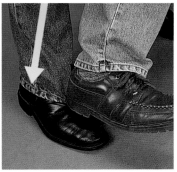 

Teeth

Biting into any part of your assailant's body will cause
severe pain and discomfort. The ears and nose are the
favourite places to go for, but any exposed skin will
do. When biting skin, 'nipping' a small area between
your teeth will greatly increase the pain inflicted.

WARNING

➤ Be wary of drawing blood if you bite an attacker
due to the (remote) possibility of HIV infection.

Head

If grabbed from the front, snap your head forward
quickly to hit your attacker's nose or lips with your
upper forehead. Use the same technique with the
back of your head if you are grabbed from behind.

USING EVERYDAY ITEMS AS WEAPONS

Ashtray

In social premises there is normally a plentiful supply of ashtrays, some of which will be fairly full. Throw the ash into the assailant's face and follow up with the ashtray itself. Most ashtrays are round in shape and irrespective of weight can be used as a Frisbee-type missile.

Baseball bat

Having a baseball bat in the house is one thing, carrying it in the street is another – this has been a favourite weapon for many a thug over the years. In any event, mark your target area with care, as the bat can easily kill your assailant. Should you find yourself confronting an assailant, and you just happen to have a baseball bat in your hand, aim for his limbs, not his head. If you are attacked in your home, concentrate on the assailant's arms, thus allowing him to escape.

Bath towel

A bath towel can be used in a variety of ways. It is best if the towel is wet, as this will add weight to the blow. One method is to use the towel like a whip, which is especially effective when used against the eyes and face. Folding the towel and twisting it into a cosh also makes a good weapon for beating strokes. Small towels can be weighted with a bar of soap.

Belt buckle

Any belt with a good metal buckle will provide a good defensive weapon. Wrap the tail end around your hand several times, then use the belt in a whipping action.  Concentrate your attack on the exposed areas of skin, e.g. the face, and neck.

Bicycle

If you are attacked while riding a bike and cannot escape, pick the bike up and use it as a shield, in the same way as you would use a chair (see below). The bicycle pump is also very handy to use in a similar way as one would use a walking stick. Should it be readily accessible, remember the bike chain was always a steadfast weapon of the old teddy-boy era in the '60s.

Boiling water

A good defence if you are attacked in your home, any hot or boiling liquid splashed in the assailant's face will allow you plenty of time to escape. Possible liquids include a cup of hot coffee or tea, or even hot soup.

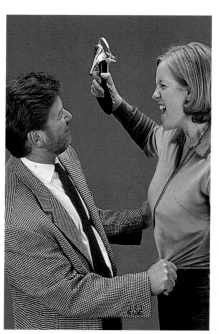

Boots and shoes

All your footwear should be comfortable, but sturdy. Kicking is one of the basic defensive moves available to you, and it's no good trying to damage an assailant in a pair of flip-flops.

A good solid boot or shoe will do damage wherever you hit your assailant. Concentrate on the assailant's legs.

AUTHOR'S NOTE

➤ When I know that I will be visiting certain parts of London, I select my shoes with care. The ones I normally favour will deliver a stunning blow, yet they are light enough for me to run in.

Bottles

For an emergency, most designs could have been made for fighting. Do not try to smash the end of the bottle off, as this normally results in the bottle disintegrating altogether. Use it as you would a club and strike for the head and temples. The body joints, such as the elbow and kneecap, are particularly good targets to hit with any bottle.

Broom

Attacks in the house can be fended off by using any type of broom. A large, wooden-headed one can be used much like a mallet, and the bristles can be

driven into the assailant's face. The broom can also be reversed, so that the handle can be used for jabbing into the solar plexus.

Chair

The household chair is a very formidable weapon. Hold it by gripping the back support with one hand and the front of the seat with the other. For attacks in the home, use the chair to keep your attacker at bay until you can position yourself close to an escape exit. Attack with a chair if your assailant has a knife. The seat of the chair works as a shield while the legs can be prodded into the assailant's head and chest.

Cigarette lighter

If you find that you are pinned down, or held from behind, by a stronger assailant, and it is feasible to reach a lighter about your person, use it. Even the strongest hold will be broken by the flame. Once you are free, grip the lighter firmly in your fist and strike against the assailant's temples.

Coat

Not so much a weapon, more of a shield. If you are attacked in the street, remove your coat and use it as a bull-fighter would do. Throwing it over the assailant's head may only give you a couple of seconds start, but you will run faster without the coat.

Coins

Filling your hand with loose pocket change and forming a fist, will greatly increase the force of any blow. Additionally, several coins tied into the corner of a handkerchief or scarf will form a very effective cosh. Use it by swinging it at the assailant's temple or general skull area.

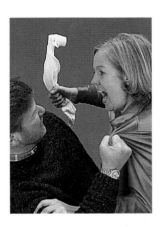

Comb

Any type of comb or hairbrush will cause discomfort if dragged quickly across the eyes. Equally, just scratching the assailant's skin will cause him to release any hold he might have on you. Some combs have a long, sharply pointed rat-tail handle which is ideal for stabbing.

Deodorant or hairspray

Many women carry some form of aerosol spray in their handbag. Use it by spraying it directly into the face of an assailant. Hair spray is particularly effective

against the eyes, or sprayed directly into the mouth or nostrils. Perfume sprays can also be used but because the aerosol pressurre is often less, you have to use it close to your assailant's face.

WARNING

➤ Some self-defence books advocate using a cigarette lighter to ignite the spray from an aerosol can. This will work, but is highly dangerous – there is more than a 50/50 chance that the can will explode in your hand.

Desktop items

A letter opener is a perfectly legitimate item in any home or office. Choose one that is substantial and has a good blade and firm handle. Use it as you would a knife. Likewise a heavy glass paperweight thrown at an assailant can cause severe damage.

Fire extinguisher

Most homes and offices now have several fire extinguishers. The pressurised contents can be used against any assailant by spraying him in the face, thus blinding him. Once your assailant is blind, you have the opportunity to escape or if circumstances require it, follow this up by beating him over the head with the metal bottle.

Golf club

Although one is not likely to be assaulted on the golf course, golf clubs in the car or the home make a very useful weapon. Hold the club by the grip and swing it at your assailant's head or hands. The long reach offered by the club allows you to strike without getting within range of any knife. Used properly, a golf club can withstand most attacks, excluding a gun.

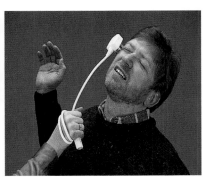

Kettle cord

Most kettles or coffee machines in the home have a one-metre length electric cable. In an emergency, disconnect the cord from both power socket and appliance and use it as a weapon. Grip the appliance end and swing the plug at your assailant; it is extremely effective against the head. The same principle can be used in the office, i.e. computer and printer leads.

Keys

Most people carry a bunch of keys. Use them by

laying the key-fob in the palm of your hand with the keys protruding between your fingers. This forms a very effective knuckle-duster. Direct your blows against the vital pressure points of the head and neck.

AUTHOR'S NOTE

➤ I have a small plastic baton fitted to my car keys, which not only stops me losing them, but offers an excellent defensive weapon.

Magazine or newspaper

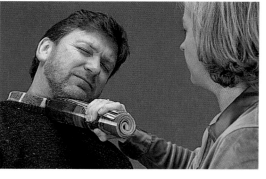

Roll any magazine into a baton and hold it by the centre to stab with, using either backward or forward thrusts.

Hold the end of the baton if you intend to beat your assailant around the head. A rolled-up newspaper is a great defensive weapon for fending off a knife attack.

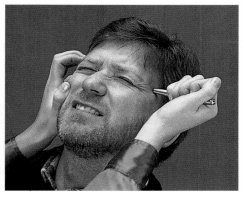

Pen

Most types of pen have a pointed tip, which means that they will penetrate the skin if used in a punching manner. Hold the pen as if it were a knife and use it against any exposed part of the assailant's body, such as the neck, wrists and temple. The harder you punch with the pen the better the results.

Pepper and curry powder

Both pepper and curry powder offer an excellent deterrent against attacks in the home. In an emergency, throw the dry contents directly into the face of your assailant. A much better idea is to fill a plant spray bottle with a rich mixture of both ingredients and water. Two ounces of each added to half a pint of warm water is a good mix. Let the contents settle for a couple of days, giving it a good shake each morning. Keep your spray in a safe but accessible place. Washing powder can be used in exactly the same way. Keep out of the reach of children.

Poker

Most homes have a poker on the fireplace, even

though in many cases it is only for decoration. The humble poker, traditionally the weapon used against the common cat burglar, is an excellent weapon. Swing it at the surface bone parts of your assailant's body, such as wrists and elbows. Be careful about using it against the head – it is possible to kill with a cast-iron poker.

Rocks and soil

If you are attacked outdoors, throwing rocks at your assailant will help keep him at bay. Closer up, a handful of sand or dirt thrown in the assailant's face will temporarily blind him.

Scissors and screwdrivers

Such items are to be found in most homes. It is even legal to carry scissors in your handbag, and a screwdriver is a common item in any car. They are best used for jabbing and stabbing. Hold and use them as you would a knife.

Socks

Silly as it may seem, a sock will make a very effective cosh. Fill it with sand, chippings or soil. In the home or street, use loose pocket change. Swing it hard at the assailant's head in the same fashion as you would use any cosh.

Torch

It is common sense to carry a torch or flashlight with you while walking out in a dark night.

Additionally, you should put torches in various places around the home for emergencies. Although expensive, the more modern Mag-light type torches are extremely good, and make an excellent weapon – the SAS have used them for years. In any attack, use the torch as you would a hammer or club.

Walking stick

This item offers excellent protection for the elderly, although it is not uncommon for hikers of all ages to carry a walking stick. The best type is one with a heavy ornate top, with a metal-tipped, strong wooden shaft. Use the walking stick as you would a fencing sword; slash, and rain blows at the assailant's head and solar plexus. Slash down hard at the wrists. It is very useful against a knife or bottle attack. You may be able to stop the assailant pursuing you if you can strike his kneecaps hard enough. It is a good idea to have a small strap securing the walking stick to your wrist.

Common Attacks

DISORDERLY CONDUCT

Disorderly conduct is basically a breach of the peace and if it goes unchecked, is a prelude to more violent action. The noise and amateur dramatics of a pub argumentmay have only have caused a breach of the peace, but the moment blows are exchanged, a more serious crime has been committed. It is at this stage that a person can find himself or herself sucked into a situation they should have avoided.

Picture yourself in a pub, when someone insults your partner. While you may retaliate verbally, you are not entitled to hit the loud-mouth. Likewise, if the insults lead to a confrontation where you decide to stand up to the loud-mouth and have a go, you are equally guilty of causing a breach of the peace by consenting to fight.

In most cases, when you are not directly involved, disorderly conduct can be anticipated. A drunk shouting his mouth off at the bar does not make a good drinking companion. Simple domestic disputes between neighbours are also to be avoided. Unless you believe a life is being threatened, the answer is to walk away.

PURSE-SNATCHING AND MUGGING

Purse-snatching is on the increase. It is a simple way for criminals to get access to your money, credit cards, address and house keys. Most purse-snatchers work as a team. They will target their intended victim and systematically tag them. It is not unusual for one of the gang to distract the victim while another grabs the bag containing the purse.

PURSE/WALLET SECURITY

➤ Carry an old purse or wallet with just a few pounds in it – no purse snatcher is going to hang around long enough to see how much he has stolen from you.

➤ Always have this dummy wallet or purse in a prominent place, include any out-of-date credit cards and cut out some paper money topped with a five-pound note.

➤ Make sure your real wallet or purse is well concealed.

➤ Never let any mugger get hold of your address, or house keys: they may be tempted to pay you a visit.

GANG ATTACKS

Most gangs are made up of teenagers, in some cases very young teenagers, and can comprise either male, female or both. Most gangs have a leader. He is the one that feels he should entertain the troops by setting an example – he is the one to watch. If you find yourself surrounded by a gang, deal with the

leader; most of the others will watch how he handles the situation. If you can convince the leader that he will get serious trouble from you, he may well decide not to have a go.

➤ Try to avoid any gang, or use other pedestrians to shield you as you pass.

➤ If confronted, keep moving; it will be hard for them to surround you.

➤ Always keep your eye open for a break in the gang – if a gap appears, go for it.

➤ If you are in immediate danger, go for the leader first.

➤ A gang will act differently with a man than with a woman (see Attacks on Women, p.143).

AUTHOR'S NOTE

➤ I have been held up by muggers twice in my life, once in the USA and once in South America. In the USA, I convinced the muggers that all I had was pocket money, and that my wallet was still in the hotel. They were so stupid that they agreed to accompany me to the hotel and get my wallet. Once at the door, I ran inside shouting for all I was worth that the guy had a gun. He was so surprised that he decided to run – he was still running when the police caught him. In South America, the three youths, all armed with knives, took my wallet and watch, with a total value around £100 – a cheap price in exchange for my life.

VIOLENT CRIMES

Guns, knives and machetes are all very dangerous and in most close attacks they will cause serious injury, or even kill. In the event of a robbery, give up your possessions without any fuss. In the event of rape or revenge, you may be given little choice and as such, forced to defend yourself. In truth, unless you are fully trained and confident in dealing with such situations, your chances are slim. The only effective response to an attack involving a knife or a gun is a gun in professional hands, i.e. the police.

WEAPONS USED IN AN ASSAULT

Knife

There are two types of knife attack:

➤ The first is committed by someone who is in dispute and a knife happens to be handy. This type of person is not likely to stab or cut you, but will use the knife in a threatening manner. This can be a good stage at which to call a halt to the conflict, by convincing the attacker of the consequences if he stabs you. This may not work, but people who are not used to fighting with a knife, will sometimes listen to reason, especially if the alternative is a long prison sentence. In some instances the attacker may use a knife to equal the odds, as he sees it, against a larger or more aggressive opponent. In this case let the aggressor know exactly what you will do with the knife if you get hold of it. Most will back down at the thought.

➤ The second type of knife attack involves someone who usually carries a knife – the degree of threat is related to the weapon and to the skill of the person using it. If you are involved in an argument with a person who carries a knife, back down. Try to avoid the situation altogether – run away if you can. They may laugh at you, but you will still be in one piece.

➤ Knives can and often do kill; if you are forced to fight carry out the following actions:

> **CONFRONTING A KNIFE ATTACKER**

➤ Look for a blocking object, such as a chair.

➤ Get some protection – a jacket or a coat around one arm.

➤ Stay away from the knife, if your attacker is slashing.

➤ If he is using a stabbing action, take the blade on a briefcase or handbag.

➤ Use a stick, broom, umbrella to parry the knife hand.

➤ Do not try to kick the knife hand; instead, go for the attacker's lower legs.

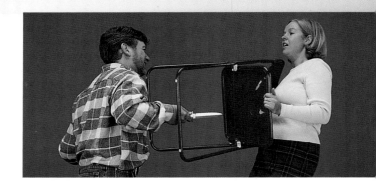

Guns

It is very difficult to offer any defence against a person holding a gun on you. If a criminal carries a gun, you have to assume that he will use it. It is true that many criminals buy a gun with no idea how to use it, and that in most cases, few people will have the

gun ready for immediate firing.

Handguns

An automatic pistol normally has a magazine which contains a certain amount of bullets. The magazine needs to be in the pistol; it normally fits inside the hand-grip. Once in position, a bullet has to be fed into the chamber of the barrel – this is done when the top slide is pulled back, cocking the pistol. From this stage, providing the safety catch is set to fire, the weapon will fire if the trigger is squeezed.

A revolver is different in as much as it houses its bullets in a round cylinder. When the trigger is pulled, a bullet is fired, and the cylinder is moved one place to the right, thus pulling a new bullet ready under the hammer.

Confronting someone with a handgun

Within the SAS there are techniques for disarming a person training a gun on you, but these take years of practice and even then there is no guarantee that they will work. In the event that you are being threatened with a gun, and your death or the death of another looks imminent, consider the following.

➤ Assess the person holding the gun: could you take him if he were unarmed

➤ Assess his actions: how close has he come to you? (A professional will keep out of striking range.)

➤ Look at the weapon: is it an automatic or a revolver? Is the firing hammer cocked back?

➤ Can you see if the safety catch is on or off?

➤ With the gunman standing in front of you, and you with your hands in the air, a straightforward downward snatch at the gun with both hands may work.

➤ Once you have a hold of the gun, grip it for all you are worth, using both hands to twist the gun away from you and toward your attacker. He will think twice before pulling the trigger.

➤ If you have good leverage on the barrel of the weapon, you may be able to wrestle it from your attacker's hands.

➤ If you get hold of the weapon, or if it falls free, kick or throw it out of range, and continue your fight on a more even basis.

Both automatics and revolvers will only fire the bullet that is in the chamber, immediately under the hammer. It is possible to prevent a second bullet being fired by holding the top slide of an automatic or gripping the cylinder of a revolver.

If the gunman has the weapon pressed into your back and you are standing still, consider adopting the following moves:

➤ Twist your body around suddenly.

➤ Use a back-fist blow to block the attacker's weapon hand.

➤ Follow through with a really aggressive action.

➤ Grip and hold the weapon hand to prevent being shot.

➤ Remove the weapon from your attacker if possible.

If you manage temporarily to disarm your attacker and you get the opportunity, put some distance between yourself and the gunman, by running away. With the threat behind you, even 20 metres will suffice; members of the SAS would find it difficult to hit a running man at this distance with a pistol. Zig-zag as you run. Do not stop even if you feel a bullet

 SAS ACTION

➤ Having been shot myself, I can tell you that the immediate effect is one of numbness, although you will still be able to operate. Take heart that some 70% of all bullet wounds are in the limbs, or non-fatal parts of the body.

hitting you; if you are seriously hit, you will go down automatically. Put at least 50 metres between yourself and the gunman: his aim may not be very good, but a lucky bullet can still kill you.

Fully automatic weapons

Although these are illegal in Britain, many fully automatic weapons find their way into the hands of criminals. In most cases these weapons are used for serious crimes, such as drug-gang hits, major robberies and terrorist activities.

If you are confronted by anyone with an automatic weapon, do exactly what they say. Do not play the hero if there are others around, as automatic weapons have the habit of firing bullets in a very haphazard way.

Defensive Moves

FIRST MOVES

If you have to fight, look for the signs when your opponent is about to strike.

Almost all attackers will telegraph their first movement by:

➤ widening their eyes,
➤ glancing sideways, or
➤ going up on their toes.

Unless your attacker is using a weapon, the first blow will almost certainly be a right hook. At the same time watch out for any incoming kick – your attacker will twist his shoulders just prior to lashing out with his foot.

THE FIRST BLOW

Concentrate on steadying yourself for your first blow. Make it
➤ sharp
➤ accurate
➤ aggressive.

Make a lot of noise as you deliver your blow. If you manage to knock your attacker to the ground, run off. If you do not, relax and prepare your next defensive move.

If at first you don't succeed... bear hug!

Should your initial attack fail to make much impression, and you find that your attacker has hit you with enough force to make you groggy, go for a bear hug. No matter how weak you are, throw your arms around him and push your head into his chest. If you do not do this, and stagger backwards, dazed but still standing, you will be an open target. Hugging your attacker will prevent him from doing you too much damage, and will give you time to recover.

Keep calm

Try hard not to lose your cool, although this is easier said than done. Don't worry either about losing control of your bladder. Peeing yourself is nothing compared to the damage that your assailant can cause.

SAS ACTION

➤ In any battle, no matter how strong the enemy, they can only front a limited amount of soldiers at one time. The secret to stopping them is to hit them hard and run.

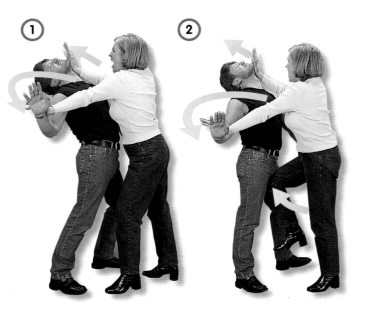

ATTACKS FROM THE FRONT

Most attacks normally start as an attack from the front. If you are quick and recognise that you are about to be attacked, take the following actions.

➤ Go into your 'on guard' stance.

➤ Block any strike with one and arm chin jab with your other hand (pic 1. above).

➤ Continue through the motion: push back your attacker's head to unbalance him.

➤ Make sure you are well balanced before bringing up your knee into his groin (pic. 2).

➤ Try to avoid the attacker holding on to you or any part of your clothing.

➤ Once free – kick, break and run.

If your attacker grabs your wrist and attempts to pull you off balance towards him, as in (pic 3 below):

➤ Kick hard to his shin just below the kneecap (pic 4).

➤ Secure his hand against your own captured wrist with your free hand and, at the same time, twist your captured hand over and back, cutting down with the edge of your hand across the back of your wrist. This will lock his wrist in a twisted position and inflict intense pain.

➤ Pull your attacker forward and down to the ground.

Attacks to the Throat

In many cases, an attacker will grab a someone around the throat using both hands to throttle them. He will generally force them to the ground, maintaining this hold. If you anticipate your attacker going for your throat, drop your chin on to your chest to prevent him from getting a stranglehold. If this is not possible, try to relax – the stranglehold on you will not be so effective. Should you find yourself threatened in this manner, take the following actions.

➤ In the early stages, when he has just gripped you, bring your right hand, fist clenched, up to your left shoulder.

➤ With a backward swing, drive a back-fist against your attacker's temple.

If this is not successful, try the folowing technique:

➤ Link your fingers together between you and your attacker (pic. 1)

➤ Raise your clenched arms in an 'A' shape above your head and drive them down onto his forearms, maintaining the 'A' by keeping your elbows lower than your hands.

➤ This will have the effect of either breaking your attacker's hold or at worst bringing his head forward.

➤ Snap your forehead down on your attacker's nose as you bring down your linked arms.

➤ This can be used standing or lying on the ground.

Another simple technique to use to escape from being grabbed with both hands around your throat is:

➤ Step back with your left foot.

➤ Draw the right after it quickly to assume the natural stance.

➤ Bring your right arm over and across his hands and swing to your left.

➤ Your left hand has meanwhile taken a hold on the nearest point, i.e. his right wrist, and therefore assisted in pulling him off balance.

ATTACKS FROM BEHIND

Coping with bear-hugs

When attacked from the rear, if the attacker's arms or hands are within range, try biting them. If you manage to get your teeth into a section of his skin, only bite a small section. By doing this you will get a better grip, and it will hurt a lot more. A small section is also easier grind your teeth into. However, remember that you may be exposed – if only to a small degree – to HIV infection if your bite draws blood from your attacker.

Bear-hugs around your waist

If your attacker has a low bear-hug hold on you, with his arms more around your waist than your chest, making it difficult for you to slip out of, try doing a rear head-butt.

➤ Push up on your toes and bend forward at the waist (pic.1 overleaf).

➤ Slam your head sharply backwards and try to hit your attacker's nose.

➤ Combine this with a backward strike from a balled fist into his groin (pic. 2).

If an attacker grabs you from behind using just one arm, take the following action.

➤ Push your body-weight forward, twisting in the opposite direction of your attacker's gripping arm.

➤ At the same time, raise your left elbow as high as possible out in front of you.

➤ Your attacker will automatically try to pull you back – use this by twisting back the opposite way, only this time use your momentum, and that of your attacker, to bring your elbow back into his face.

This move can be combined with a backward blow from your other hand, driving your balled fist into his testicles.

Bear hugs pinning your arms by your side

If you are grabbed from behind in a bear-hug with both your arms pinned at your side, try the following manoeuvres to break the hold.

➤ Bend your backside into the attacker, at the same time link your hands together.

➤ Bend your knees to drop your body height, try to slip down through the bear-hug (pic.1 below).

➤ With your hands linked, swing your elbows up and outwards.

➤ Using a rocking, twisting-type movement, swing from the hips, driving your elbow into your attacker's stomach (pic. 2 above).

➤ Follow through with a back head-butt or back instep foot stamp.

➤ Once free – kick, break and run.

Hair holds from the rear

If your attacker seizes you by the hair from behind, and pulls you backwards, carry out the following actions:

➤ Step back with him.

➤ Use both your hands to grip your attacker's wrist.

➤ Turn inwards, facing your opponent.

➤ Step back as far as possible, and jerk your attacker's hand off your head. This may cause your hair to be torn out by the roots, but it is most probable that you won't notice until later.

➤ Still gripping your opponent's wrist, pull him towards you bringing up your knee to meet his groin.

FORCED AGAINST A WALL

In some cases, your attacker may block you against a wall and wait a few seconds before having a go at you. Should your attacker at any time present himself side-on to you, or you can manoeuvre yourself into this position, take the following action.

➤ Grab the crown of his hair and pull his head sharply back. This will not only unbalance your attacker, but will expose his throat

➤ Bring your fist down onto his windpipe with one hard blow.

➤ If you continue to pull backwards, your attacker should drop to the ground.

➤ If your attacker has no hair to

grip, use your hand like a claw and grab at his nose and eyes, forcing his head backwards.

➤ Once free – kick, break and run.

SAS ACTION

➤ There is an old saying in the SAS: 'Take hold of a man's hair and the body will follow.' The secret is maintaining your grip from the rear; never let your opponent twist around to face you..

DEFENDING YOURSELF ON THE GROUND

During any conflict, there is a good chance that you will be knocked to the ground. You will be very vulnerable, but do not give up. If you are hit hard to the head, particularly on the point of the jaw, you will probably be feeling fairly groggy. Concentrate on maintaining your determination and stamina to continue – that should see you through the pain. Learning the art of falling is almost as important as staying on your feet. It is something that needs practice and falling on mats in the gym is vastly different from being thrown on to the road or on rough ground.

Let us presume that your assailant has been able to knock you down. He leans over you, grabbing you by the throat, with you lying flat on your back.

➤ Use your left hand to grab his right wrist.

➤ Bending your right leg, draw your shin-bone underneath his right armpit.

➤ Pull hard on his right arm. At the same time, raise your left leg, taking it over his head and in front of his face until your calf is brought against his throat.

➤ Straighten up your body, applying a straight arm lock, the fulcrum being formed by your crutch.

➤ Trap his arm firmly held between your thighs, applying extreme pressure at the elbow joint.

➤ Once this lock is successfully applied there is no escape from it whatever, no matter how powerful or experienced your opponent is. It is possible to break the arm in this position.

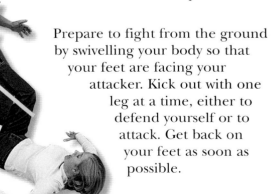

Prepare to fight from the ground by swivelling your body so that your feet are facing your attacker. Kick out with one leg at a time, either to defend yourself or to attack. Get back on your feet as soon as possible.

Getting up from the ground

Once down, you become vulnerable, but not helpless, but my advice is to get up as soon as possible. The following is an easy method for getting up from the ground. All moves should be in one continuous roll or twist of your body:

➤ Turn over sharply on to your left side, with your stomach facing downwards.

➤ Place both palms on the ground and push, at the same time tucking your right knee under your body (pic.1 above).

➤ Swing your left leg under your body until your foot is flat on the ground. (pic.2).

➤ Spring up, turn to face your attacker.

➤ Adopt the 'on guard' position.

An alternative method is similar to what we see in a lot of movies, but with a little practice it will work.

➤ Roll on to your back.

126

➤ Bring your knees up to your chest and over your head in a rocking motion.

➤ Rock forwards using a rolling action.

➤ Favour either your left or right hand, palm down to spring back on to your feet.

➤ Face your attacker.

➤ Adopt the 'on guard' position.

KICKING

Most people see confrontation as a form of fist fight, but it is vital to understand that the legs can be a far more powerful weapon. A kick with the edge of a shoe or boot against your attacker's legs will cause a great deal of pain.

Kicking, like fist-fighting, requires practice. If you have made a makeshift punch bag, lower it until it is a few inches off the ground. Now practice several kicking techniques.

Techniques to practice

Straight kick

➤ Stand about one metre away from the bag, in the 'on guard' position.

➤ Try a straight kick, as if you were aiming for an attacker's knee.

➤ Concentrate on your speed and surprise, your balance and your recovery.

➤ Use your arms to help control your balance, and step back.

Repeat this until you are confident in the move. If you find that your balance is off, it means you are kicking too high.

Grazing kick

➤ Step in closer to the bag, raise your foot and drag it hard down the side of your punch bag.

➤ Finish up by stamping your foot hard down to

practise stamping on your attacker's feet.

This grazing action, combining with a sharp blow to the toes, can be very painful, and is a good technique to try if you are being held by an attacker.

Kneeing your attacker

For a third option, again move in close and try hitting the top of your punch-bag with your knee. Once more the element of speed and surprise are vital. Drive your knee up as if you were running on the spot; balance is difficult at this stage as your feet will be close together. Use your hands to push away your attacker.

If you are being forced upstairs

You may find yourself being attacked on or near steps or stairs. If you are being chased up a flight of steps or a rapist is forcing you up into the bedroom, carry out the following actions.

➤ Get in front of your attacker.

➤ Wait until you are near the top, then bend down and grip the top step or handrail.

➤ As you lean forward to do this, kick back with your foot to knock your attacker down the stairs.

➤ If you are at home, run for the bathroom, lock yourself in and shout for help.

BATON TECHNIQUES

The baton is a rod-like instrument that is normally just over half an inch in diameter and some 5 or 6 inches in length. Its outer surface can be plain, or machined with grooves or ridges to provide better grip. Some are fitted with a standard key-ring end. The baton may look innocent, but when used properly, it can get you out of a lot of nasty situations because, in spite of its small size, it is capable of inflicting pain and pressure when used correctly.

If used properly, the baton will allow for a certain amount of control over any assailant, without causing serious damage or injury. It is most effective when used against the surface bone areas of the body, such as the skull, the arms and lower legs.

Holding the baton

There are several different ways of holding the baton:

➤ The end grip allows the baton to be used as one would use a knife.

➤ The middle grip allows for both ends to be used in a swinging action.

➤ The thumb grip allows hammer-type blows to be struck.

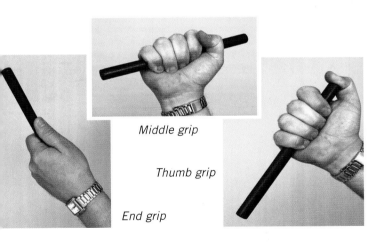

Middle grip

Thumb grip

End grip

Basic blocking movements with the baton

High blocks

If an assailant swings towards your head, then use a high block. This is done by holding the baton in the thumb grip and swinging out in a radius from your

131

High block

forehead to the assailant's approaching inner arm. It is of little consequence where the baton makes contact, as the result will be painful enough to stop the assault.

Middle blocks

Middle blocks are used when the assailant attacks

Middle block

your torso. Several different thrusts can be used. Striking the abdomen in a frontal or rear movement will cause the assailant to drop to the ground. It is also possible to hit at the throat, solar plexus or testicles.

Low blocks

Low blocks are used to counter kicking attacks by an assailant. Block the kick with your free hand and, using the thumb grip, drive the baton into the leg anywhere from the crutch down to the

Low block

foot. The inner kneecap is a particularly good point to strike.

Using the baton to break a hold

Front hold

If you are gripped by an assailant from the front, the best method of release is to drive the baton up into the assailant's throat. Alternatively, drive the baton down into the spot where the neck meets the shoulders.

Rear hold

When gripped from behind, use the baton against the metacarpal bones on the back of your assailant's hands. Several short sharp jabs will guarantee your release.

Forcing the baton down on an assailant's wrist using both hands while applying pressure to the underside of his wrist with your thumbs will release any frint grip on you.

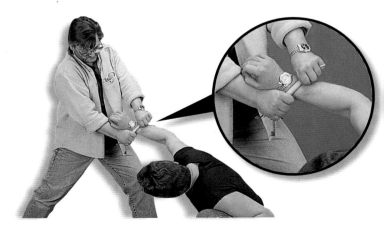

SELF-DEFENCE IN SOCIAL SITUATIONS

Groping

Women find that some men may molest them while in a crowded place, such as a disco. A 'get your hands off me' will normally do the trick, but if the person persists, and it is feasible to grab hold of his hand, try the following action.

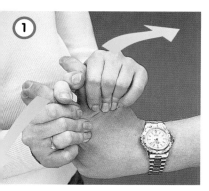

➤ Grab his hand by the fingers and split them, two of his fingers in each of your hands (pic. 1).

➤ At the same time bend his wrist and push him back off balance (pic. 2).

➤ With control of his hand, twist him to one side and force him to the floor (pic. 2).

➤ When you have him on the floor, maintain your

finger grip and (pic. 3) stamp down hard on his groin.

Dealing with aggressive drunks

Drunks can also be a nuisance at parties and discos, and for some reason they like to hang around your neck. They can easily be disposed of by the following steps.

➤ With the drunk's arm around your neck, place your near-side leg behind the drunk and between his legs.

136

➤ Place your elbow onto his chest and push backwards (pic. 2).

(2)

➤ Twist your body around as he falls over backwards and either walk away or, if necessary, kick him in the testicles (pic. 3).

(3)

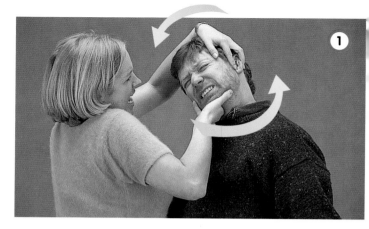

Head holds

Another method of getting rid of an over-friendly
drunk is to grab hold of his head. By twisting the
head about on his shoulders you can easily
disorientate a drunk.

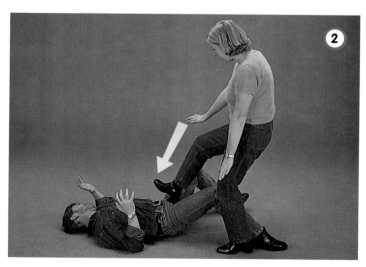

➤ Reach up and dig your fingers into his head and get the best hold you can; for example, fingers on the ears, or up the nose.

➤ Twist the head about in a circular, shaking motion.

Forcing an over-friendly drunk's head back while tripping him with your leg will break his grip on you.

➤ Drop his head to one side and he should fall to the floor. Stamp on him if necessary.

Using your bottle

Drinking directly from the bottle now seems the in thing to do, and many people do it. Beer bottles can also be useful if you find yourself being hassled at a party or in a pub.

➤ At the first opportunity, grab your antagonist's wrist, and pull the arm upward.

➤ Grip the bottle around its middle and ram the neck up into his armpit. This produces dramatic results, as the arm will go numb.

SECURING AN ASSAILANT

If you have restrained an assailant, and with the help of others have managed to hold him, your first priority is to make sure he will do no further damage. Use boot or shoe laces to tie his hands and his waist belt to secure his feet. In the event that neither are available, make the assailant sit on his hands, palms up. Undo his trousers and pull them down to his ankles.

In the home, use anything at hand to bind and secure the assailant; cling film is excellent. Several good turns around the wrists will prevent him from doing any further damage, but likewise will do no damage to him.

Clingfilm is a particularly effective restraint

Attacks on Women

AUTHOR'S NOTE

➤ I have given much thought to this section of the book, and I have taken advice from many women on how they would react in a violent situation. The after-effect of surviving a violent rape or serious assault can be magnified by guilt, especially when there has been no attempt to fight back. No woman should try to understand the psychology of why a man is attacking her. He will have no real remorse.

➤ Surprise is the best defence and, given the right instruction, a woman can actively defend herself. To this end it is vital that you study the self-defence techniques in this book.

WOMEN AND SELF-DEFENCE

With regard to women and self-defence, much has been made of the presumed differences between men and women. A woman's ability to fend off an attacker is generally thought to be less than that of a man, partly due to the belief that the size and physical strength of a man will be greater than that of a woman, and the tradition that the man is the protector. In fact size and strength do not necessarily determine a person's ability to themselves – small women have been known to successfully fight off bigger and stronger attackers.

Many women are fitter, brighter and quicker than their male counterparts. They do not drink as much and therefore have better reasoning behaviour in any conflict. The most notable difference between the sexes, in the context of this book, is the psychological programming of children from the moment they enter this world. Boys are expected to be tough, to fight back at bullies whereas girls are expected not to fight back. This type of conditioning is partially responsible for women being viewed not only by men, but by their own sex, as victims.

Believe in yourself

Women need to overcome their fear of fighting. They have great reserves of anger and positive energy within them and they should be prepared to use their strengths to keep themselves safe in violent situations. It is simply a matter of belief in themselves; there is nothing to lose and everything to gain.

React immediately

In order to shock an attacker and cause him to lose his confident edge, a woman should act quickly and decisively. Trust your instincts in such situations and act on them but it is of vital importance not to delay your response – the element of surprise cannot be overemphasised because you can disarm an attacker if you do something he does not expect.

DO THE UNEXPECTED

➤ Show confidence. Do not let the attacker exert his violence by observing apparent weaknesses on your part. Weakness is all about perception and your psychological strength will have an effect on the attacker.

➤ Counter-attack if rushed upon. Yelling, running, punching and kicking are all effective means of defence.

DOMESTIC VIOLENCE

Any violent attack inside the home is a criminal offence. Men and women do not have the right to

abuse each other, either physically or emotionally. Unfortunately, many women experience abuse from their husbands or partners for many years. This abuse may last for years, usually until the woman leaves. Women may stay with a violent partner for many reasons – lack of money, threats, a belief that he will change – but it is important that they should realise that there are places they can go where they will receive advice, accomodation and support: contacts for women's aid centres and other refuges can be found in telephone directories or obtained from your local social services department.

In the early stages, women experiencing domestic violence may not acknowledge their experiences as abuse. However, at some point they should consider making some arrangements to leave. This is not an easy decision to make, especially if children are involved. If you have reached this point, tell a female friend of your troubles, and that you might need to stay. Pack a small overnight bag and leave it with her. Put away enough money to pay for a night's bed and breakfast, and add to this a list of women's crisis centres which can be found in your local telephone book or obtained from Women's Aid. If feasible, ask neighbours to call the police if they hear sounds of any disturbance.

Domestic violence is a crime against women and needs to be reported. If your husband or partner continues to be violent, take action. The courts will help, and it is possible to get a court injunction preventing your partner from coming near you.

GANG ATTACKS

For a woman, being alone and confronted by a male gang is probably one of the worst scenarios imaginable. Simple self-confidence should be your first defence in this situation, since by not reacting as they expect of a woman, the gang may give up on you. The more determination you have to win through, the more it will unnerve your attackers.

Dealing with the gang

The key element in dealing with this situation is to quickly establish who the gang leader is and concentrate on him; he will either be the biggest or the one doing all the talking.

➤ You should make eye contact with the leader and hold it.

➤ By being self-confident and continuing to move forward while quietly but firmly asking the attacker to get out of your way, you may well convince the leader to back down.

➤ If he breaks eye contact, you should carry on moving forward and out of his gang.

➤ Should he still block your way, close in on him, but maintain some space between you, all the while holding eye contact.

➤ Try not to allow yourself to be surrounded.

At this point, there is always the possibility he will act as if it was all a joke and let you pass, with a terse laugh or comment. If this approach doesn't work, consider using your voice to draw attention to yourself and your predicament; the gang is unlikely to want a woman sceaming at them, and yelling can give an added dimension to any physical attack that may be necessary.

In the last resort, if the gang attacks, go for it. Use all your skills – voice, punches and kicks – and run at the first opportunity if there is space to get away.

Listed below are the important points to remember.

➤ Maintain eye contact.

➤ Do not be distracted from your chosen course of exit.

➤ Do not talk to the attackers except to issue orders.

➤ Protect your back – it is more difficult to face a victim than to attack from behind.

STALKING

In recent years there has been an upsurge in what the media have termed 'stalking'. This term is normally given to people who are infatuated with someone and who relentlessly follow them around.

However, stalkers are often not content simply to stalk their subject: physical assaults and written or verbal abuse all feature in what is often a clear show of power, intimidation and violence.

Stalking and the police

If you believe that you are being stalked, it is worth contacting the police. However, be aware that the time of this book going to press, there is no

legislation dealing with a specific crime of stalking; at the moment the police can treat stalking as a breach of the peace or as an offence under Section 5 of the Public Order Act which requires proof that you have suffered alarm or distress as a result. Inevitably, therfore, unless a physical assault occurs, a swift remedy to your concerns that someone is following you may not be forthcoming.

If you believe you are being followed

Safe havens

If you are away from your normal environment, and you feel you are being followed, no matter what the reason, look for a safe haven. You may just be seeing shadows, but it is always better to be safe rather than sorry. Try to identify possible safe havens as you walk around the streets, for example, well-occupied buildings, such as police stations, public buildings, hospitals, banks, hotels and shops. If you feel immed-

iately threatened, simply walk to the nearest house with the light on and request the use of their phone.

When walking along the pavement, walk in the middle of the pavement and be alert to alley openings or recessed shop doorways. If you think someone is tailing you, simply turn around and check. Cross the street (twice if necessary) to see if you are being followed. If you are not sure, go into a large store or similar safe haven and phone for a taxi to take you home or to your destination. If your assailant follows you in, tell a shop employee or phone a friend. If you are ever personally confronted, the first thing to do is face your attacker: you will then be able to see him and what he is doing.

➤ Try not to take short-cuts through unknown or lonely areas.

➤ Carry a personal alarm and have it ready for use.

➤ If possible, when going home late at night, ring someone at home to watch for your arrival.

➤ Ask the friend or the taxi driver who drops you off to wait until you have opened your front door.

➤ Carry your keys in your hand. Don't stand at your front door searching for them in your handbag or pockets.

➤ Walk towards the oncoming traffic – this way no one can pull up behind you.

AUTHOR'S NOTE

➤ I have often found myself in parts of London and Liverpool where there have been several groups of youths blocking the pavement. Without drawing attention to myself, I have crossed the road with the pretence of looking in a shop window. This not only avoids direct confrontation, but also provides me with a mirror to watch their actions. If they seem harmless, then I proceed, staying on the opposite pavement. This arm's-length principle is one you should always adopt.

RAPE

Rape is a very common crime and can leave women's lives in ruins. More than 85% of the rapes committed are carried out by attackers that know their victim and it is not just the isolated single woman that suffers: half of all rapes are carried out by long-term partners or husbands. Rape is about the abuse of power rather than about sex per se and many rapes go unreported because the victim feels dirty and embarrassed or because they feel they will not be believed by the police or the courts. It is important to remember that rape is never the woman's responsibility or fault. Premeditation plays little part in rape cases and most are opportunistic; sometimes they can also be racially motivated.

Confronting a potential rapist

How you get out of a potential rape situation may depend on your relationship with your attacker and also on your character. You may have no hesitancy about punching a stranger but may not be able to do so to a partner (perhaps for fear of future repercussions). You may be able to talk yourself out of a situation but be prepared to use physical force if you have to: it has been shown that women who fight potential rapists escape safely more often than those who do not.

➤ Assess your attacker: How big is he? Is he drunk? Is he a mugger who sees raping you as an extra opportunity?

➤ Adopt a calm attitude and fighting stance.

➤ Use your voice: yell and draw attention to yourself.

➤ Maintain eye contact.

➤ Try not to let him touch you.

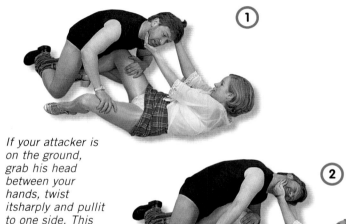

If your attacker is on the ground, grab his head between your hands, twist it sharply and pull it to one side. This will unbalance him and may provide an opening for escape

Fight back

Your attacker may not be deterred by the more subtle actions described above. If this is the case, then be prepared to fight to stop him. Your attacker will be vulnerable at points during a rape (e.g. when he is unzipping) and you should judge when the best time to attack is, if this becomes necessary.

Unless the attacker is holding a weapon to your throat, use every means at your disposal to fight him off – you can do little to make the situation any worse. Scratch, bite and kick. Rip at his hair, pull at his testicles, gouge out some of his skin. If this does not stop him, make sure you can identify him later.

Date or acquaintance rape

'Date rape' is a catchy,trivialising phrase that has arrived from America to describe this serious offence.

Generally referring to couples on a date for the first time, or early on in a relationship, date rape normally takes place when the man has not read the signs correctly and sexually assaults the woman.

A man must understand that while scoring on a first date may well increase his standing with his mates, without the full consent of the woman involved, such actions constitute rape. At the same time, the woman must understand that inviting a man she doesn't know well into her home, probably late at night and after a few drinks, may be giving her date the wrong set of signals. That said, an invitation to coffee or a drink or some intimacy in no way means a women consents to having sex forced upon her.

A man and a woman go out together because they generally like each other. The question is, how far do we commit ourselves? That can only be answered in one way – through respect, and a clear understanding of each other's signals.

➤ Keep the first date simple.

➤ Arrive and depart arranging your own transport.

➤ Dress sensibly.

➤ Be careful of the information you give out, such as address, phone number, workplace, etc.

➤ Make your intentions clear.

➤ If you don't want to have sex, say no and be prepared to back it up with force if need be.

If you have been raped

If you have been raped, report it immediately; if your first instinct is not to go to the police, you will find help, sympathetic support and advice at your local Rape Crisis centre (whose details will be in the telephone directory).

Recovering from an assault

As soon as it is safe to do so, seek help from the first reliable source. Go to the nearest police station. Seek immediate medical attention, but do not wash yourself prior to being examined. The desire to wash and change your clothes will be overwhelming, but the police will need all the evidence they can get in order to apprehend and convict your attacker. You can call a friend or relative to sit with you.

Rape crisis centres can be found in most cities, and

they help the victim through the trauma of examination and questioning. It is in your interest to be examined, not just to repair any physical damage, but also to check for pregnancy and sexually transmitted diseases. At times it may seem like you are the guilty one, but remember that the police must conduct themselves according to the law. They may ask you questions that you do not like, but try to answer them as best you can. You can have someone with you during any questioning.

If you have been raped by a friend or a relative, the courts can order that that person (including your husband) be banned from having further contact with you. Your anonymity should also be protected, if the case come to court.

HOW MEN CAN HELP

Men must realise that many women become nervous when they are alone, especially in a strange environment.

➤ Try not to walk too close behind a woman on a dark night or in an isolated spot.

➤ Don't sit too close on public transport late at night.

➤ If you see a woman in trouble, go to her aid, or get help.

MALICIOUS TELEPHONE CALLS

The telephone is normally regarded as an aid,

especially when we are in trouble, but at times it can be used by others for intimidation. The simple way to avoid unwanted calls in the home is to have your telephone number made ex-directory although this would not protect you from malicious callers who dial randomly at first.

Some calls are just nuisance calls: this can happen when your telephone number is similar to the local taxi service or Chinese take-away. However, there are some people in society that get their kicks from making malicious telephone calls and it is these obscene telephone calls that are potentially dangerous. They can cause annoyance, inconvenience or anxiety. The call may come from a person you know, or from someone with whom you have a dispute.

GENERAL PHONE PRECAUTIONS

In order to minimise the problems that you could face:

➤ Do not answer the phone with your name or phone number.

➤ Do not put your name, number or messages such as 'I am not at home at the moment' on your answering machine.

Dealing with malicious calls

If you receive what you think is a malicious call, take the following action.

➤ If the caller is silent, do not try to coax the caller into speaking – simply replace the handset.

➤ Stay calm: a genuine caller, or a friend having a bit of fun, will normally speak first.

➤ Do not start telling the caller how sick they are – they want this reaction.

➤ Do not be tempted to give out any details on the phone, unless you trust the caller.

If the caller persists, contact British Telecom (call 150, free of charge) Depending on the type of nuisance call, BT will advise you on the most suitable action to take. In addition to the advice you get by calling 150, BT also offer a free-phone advice line: 0800 666 700. On BT's digital exchanges, it is possible to identify the number of your last caller by dialling 1471 although it is possible for callers to avoid being traced in this way.

In extreme cases, BT offer a specialist service, also on a free-phone number: 0800 661 441. Your call will be taken by specially trained investigators. They will use their knowledge and experience to help solve your problem, to the point where they will have the police trace your calls. Making a malicious call is a criminal offence.

DEVICES FOR PERSONAL PROTECTION

Personal alarms

There are many different types of personal alarms on the market, some good and some totally useless. It all comes down to how piercing the noise is: the more unbearable, the better. They are normally operated by either a battery or a small gas cylinder; the gas-type models will have a louder blast, but they only work for a short time, in which case a battery model may prove better. Some personal alarms now come with several features, all designed to aid you against an attacker. For example, it is possible to get a combined torch and alarm. Better still, some alarms can be fitted to your handbag or even to the back of your front door, and are activated when someone tries to steal your handbag or break in through the door. Personal alarms are available from most DIY stores, or electronic outlets.

If you have an alarm, use it. Keep it with you at all times and make sure you can reach it quickly it in an emergency: any alarm, however good, will no use if it is buried at the bottom of a bag. However, you must not rely on your personal alarm to summon help; it may well surprise your attacker, but the general public may not respond, as we get so used to alarms going off. Shout for help at the same time, and be prepared to defend yourself.

Commercial Sprays and Stun Guns

Do not be tempted to use or carry a commercially

Defence sprays

*The Mighty Zapper
stun gun*

manufactured spray or electronic stun device. Although they are approved in some countries, in many others they are banned and possession is an offence. In any case sprays are not really effective unless used in large does. Those that spray tear gas (alphachloroacetophenone) are only effective if you can get in close. The other gas commonly used is CS gas (orthochlorobenzylidene malononitrile; a strong micropulverized irritant) which is similar to that used by the military. This gas irritates the mucous linings of the nose, throat and eyes, and if used in concentrated doses, it will also affect the skin.

Stun guns, as well as being illegal in some countries, can be a double-edged weapon anyway. Most are designed to give the attacker an electric shock, however, if your assailant happens to have a weak heart you may just kill them. There are several types of stun gun on the market, some will fire a dart-type projectile which once embedded in the skin will conduct the flow of power through the body. Others have two prongs which need to be pushed against the assailant in order to complete the circuit. The shock from most stun guns is sufficient to make an adult back off, but it would be easy enough for a determined and skilled assailant to wrestle it from you, which would then mean that you would be on the receiving end.

Other devices

Remember that there are a wide variety of everyday objects (such as combs, perfume sprays, etc.) that would be legitimate objects to carry with you and which could be used to defend yourself from an attacker (see the sections on everyday objects used as weapons, p90, and also that on key-fob batons, p.130). However, it cannot be stressed too heavily that if you do use such objects in self-defence, you will be required to justify your actions subsequently to the police.

It is very difficult to offer any defence against a person holding a gun on you. If a criminal carries a gun, you have to assume that he will use it. It is true that many criminals buy a gun with no idea how to use it, and that in most cases, few people will have the gun ready for immediate firing.

Protecting Your Property

Most definitions of self-defence restrict themselves to defence of the person against attack. However, it is possible to interpret 'self-defence' in a wider context by applying many of the general principles underlying the philosophy of self-defence of your person, to that of your property, in order to counter the many hazards, natural or otherwise, that can befall the modern home.

SECURITY IN THE HOME

In a perfect world we should all feel safe in our own homes but the reality of modern urban living is that we are exposed to a real threat of criminal activity directed against our property. Theft is on the increase, and in some areas it has reached epidemic proportions. It is not just the removal of your goods that is at stake: there is also feeling of violation when the security of your home has been breached.

Make an assessment of the threat in your own area: for example, a large town with a high unemployment rate, will generally have a higher crime rate than a more rural setting. Burglars also differ: some will look for an easy target, while some will assess the benefits of robbing a house based on the rewards. In either case it is possible to make your home less liable to attack, either by creating the impression that there is nothing worth stealing, or by making it difficult for the burglar to gain entry.

SAS ACTION

➤ Most burglars will carry out some kind of reconnaissance prior to breaking into a house. This may be a simple walk past or they may actually approach the house from a discreet angle. Where an SAS soldier would ascertain how many people where living in the house by simply checking out the clothesline, a burglar would make his assessment against other objects: it could be the type of car parked in the drive or the fitments to the outside of the house and garden – all these small details add up to give an idea of the amount of wealth held in a home.

Simple ways of protecting your home

Many burglaries can be prevented by fitting good locks to doors and windows, and fitting a good alarm system. A burglar has to enter your home through

either a door or a window. Most do not like breaking the glass, mainly because of the noise factor, but they will 'jemmy' away silently at the wood surround to gain entry.

Fitting simple deadlocks is one of the cheapest and best ways of securing your home; burglars certainly don't like them. There are many types of different locks on the market – no matter what type of door or window your house has, your local DIY store should offer a good

choice. Before fitting your locks and bolts, it is advisable to think about who will to have access to your home. Some locks can be complicated to use and may inhibit some of the younger or older family members.

In addition to your locks, a front and rear door-chain can be very helpful. This will allow you to open the door a few inches to speak to people.

SAS ACTION

➤ While serving in Northern Ireland, I was often tasked to break into various premises for security reasons. To aid me in this I used a very good set of lock-picks purchased in the USA. Although I became quite adept at opening the locks, I found my biggest barrier was an old fashioned deadbolt.

Keys

Keys are important: losing them can cause you a great deal of inconvenience. Having a spare key can sometimes solve the problem, but be careful who you give it to.

➤ Don't leave spare keys outside in an obvious place – give them to a neighbour.

➤ Never tag your keys with your address.

➤　　If you do lose your keys, change the locks.

Alarm systems

Fitting an alarm to your home is by far the surest way of stopping a burglar. The main problem is choosing the right alarm for you. Most systems work from a control box which activates and de-activates the alarm to your requirements. This unit is normally fitted close to the entry and exit point of your home. From this control box a series of sensors and other devices are fitted around the house. If the alarm is triggered, a siren goes off from a visible box which is normally sited on the front of the house, while a light flashes at the same time.

Purchase a reliable unit that is simple to use (for kids as well as adults) and one that is flexible enough to adapt to your personal requirements. Always get at least two quotes for your system; these are normally free and you can compare what each security surveyor recommends. Ask them to explain how the system will work and why they feel a device should be placed in a room and its location. A basic house alarm operates with a number of components.

Control unit

The control unit is normally close to the main entry and exit point of the house, for example, the front door. This is basically the on/off switch for the system and can be operated by a key, although a four-figure combination code-number is better. The system allows time for you to exit the house once the alarm is set, and to enter the house to shut the system down. More modern control boxes will allow for different combinations of security. For example, it is possible to deactivate certain sensors so that you can pass freely through that part of the house; this is particularly good if you want to protect the downstairs while you are sleeping upstairs. A second, smaller control box can be fitted in the master bedroom to operate the system.

Magnetic switches

Magnetic switches are used on doors and windows and they are activated when the contact, which is in two halves, is broken. They are not particularly effective and a professional thief can easily get past one. They are normally used on the entry door as a clear way of activating the control box.

Vibration detectors

Vibration detectors work on a sudden change in the air. A breaking window or someone banging something that vibrates will set off the alarm. They are sensitive and can be activated by the passing of heavy traffic or movement on nearby train lines.

Movement sensors

Movement sensors, which detect movement within a given distance, are widely used for detecting burglars and intruders. Depending on the type used and where they are situated, they will cover a room or space. Providing the alarm system is set, they will

NEIGHBORHOOD CRIME WATCH

We immediately report all SUSPICIOUS PERSONS and activities to our Police Dept.

activate when anyone enters their cover pattern. Each sensor has a pattern similar to a fan and also has a depth range which can be adjusted to make allowances for animals, etc. Movement sensors are best fitted in the corner of a room, but not facing a large window. The only problem with this type of sensor is that it will not activate until the house has been breached.

Panic buttons

Panic buttons are cheap and easy to fit into any alarm system. Once the button is pushed, the alarm activ-ates. They are best used by the front door or fitted by the bed. In an emergency, an elderly or seriously ill person can activate the alarm to call for help.

Remote calling

It is possible to have your alarm system linked up to a central monitoring station. When the alarm is activated the monitoring station will confirm with you that it is not a false alarm, or they will send call out a 'key-holder' to investigate. (Note: the police will not normally respond to a house alarm going off, unless there is positive proof that a burglar may be on the premises. This is no reflection on the police; the reason is simply the high number of false alarms.) It is possible to install a remote dialling unit connected to your alarm system; this can be programmed with four private numbers of your mobile phone, works number, friends and family. In some ways this is a much better idea as it generally gets a quicker response time. If you attend such a call, do not enter the premises if you think the burglar may still be inside.

The elderly

It is unfortunate that many elderly people become the victim of an assault, a crime made worse by their lesser ability to fight back. Many criminals prey on the elderly, believing that they have hidden stores of money or valuables. Many elderly people only to

venture out in the daytime, and even then the trip is often brief. For this reason many criminals attack the elderly in their homes. Usually, the assault is for monetary gain, although many elderly women have been raped. In many cases where the attackers have not found sufficient wealth, they have beaten the elderly in the hope of locating some imaginary stash.

There is no end to the amount of scams some criminals will go to in order to con old people out of their savings, and the transgressors are not all men – many are women or even children. If you feel threatened, and you have the resources, consider installing an alarm. Check and double-check the identity of all workmen, or people who request access to your home.

➤ Never answer the door to strangers without first confirming their identity.

➤ Do not immediately believe any story you're told by an unknown caller; for example, that the slates have fallen off the back of your roof and they can repair the damage.

➤ Fit some form of panic button by your front door.

➤ Keep your savings in a bank or building society.

➤ If you are still active, carry a walking stick or long umbrella.

➤ If your means allow it, consider keeping a dog: they are great company, and are excellent early-warning alarms.

➤ Foster good relations between yourself and your family and neighbours.

BURGLARY AND UNLAWFUL ENTRY

Most homes are robbed during the daytime or when the house is unoccupied. It is easy for a burglar to

assess the daily pattern of a family: husband goes to work; wife takes the children to school then goes to work or shopping – half the houses in the country are empty between 9 a.m. and 11 a.m.

The burglar will normally choose a route to his break-in point where he cannot be seen. That is to say, he will approach from a blind side, normally at the back of the house. However, in some older houses where a recessed outer porch provides sufficient cover, it is also possible that he may force the front door. Where the house provides little cover from view, the burglar may attack your home in a swift smash and grab, for example, by throwing a brick through the window nearest to the goods, like the video recorder or television, that the burglar is after.

BURGLARS' CHIEF TARGETS

➤ Money and jewellery.

➤ Televisions and videos.

➤ Stereo systems.

➤ Antiques.

➤ Luxury goods, i.e. cameras, computers, etc.

➤ Credit cards and cheque books.

AUTHOR'S NOTE

➤ Some years ago I was helping out at an RAF open day. The stand was busy, and it was hard to keep an eye out for petty theft. However, two youths came on the stand and it was obvious that they intended to steal, so I deliberately turned my back to serve another customer. When I turned around both youths were trotting off laughing to each other. I gave chase and grabbed both,

(contd)

> ➤ forcing them to the ground. A quick search revealed that they had stolen a £20 jacket from my stand, and several other items of equal value from others. While we waited for the police to arrive, I stood holding the pair, shouting at the top of my voice that these two were thieves. Their embarrassment at being publicly humiliated was far worse for them than any sentence they were later given.

If you hear a burglar enter your home

➤ If at night, switch on the lights.

➤ Press any panic alarms that are close by.

➤ Go to any sleeping children and stay with them.

➤ If you are alone, lock the door to your room if it has one or go to a room with a locking door, such as the bathroom.

➤ Try to phone the police, and phone your nearest friend (the police can take some time to react) .

➤ Arm yourself (see Using Everyday Items as Weapons, p. 90) but...

➤ Do not confront the burglar.

➤ Often he will try to make a quick exit – do not try to block his path.

➤ Do not try to prevent him from taking your possessions.

➤ Make a note of the burglar's appearance and dress, if you see them.

➤ Note any vehicle involved, if you see it.

If you arrive home to find a burglar

➤ Do not go in the house if you suspect that someone is inside.

➤ Call for help from a neighbour's house.

➤ Do not disturb intruders. If you do, get out of their way.

➤ Do not touch anything until the police arrive.

Remember: most burglars will run the moment they feel exposed in any way.

HOUSE FIRE

Fire in the home is a real threat, and it can happen at anytime. Treat all fires as your enemy – they kill people.

Fire needs three things – ignition, fuel and oxygen. A source of ignition can be a spark or heat of some kind. That ignition source needs to apply itself to fuel – basically anything that will burn; the more

combustible the material, the quicker the fire will start. Although ignited fuel can burn by itself, the third ingredient, oxygen, will really feed the flames. Take away any of these three ingredients and the fire will die.

Once lit, a fire is self-sustaining, providing it has both fuel and air. Trap the fire in a room or confined space and the temperature will rise until the flames reach flash-over point. This is where the fire will consume everything in its path. Flash-over normally occurs when a large house fire is given a huge blast of air, such as opening an outside door or window.

The speed of a fire can be tremendous, and a whole house can be engulfed in minutes. People trapped in a house fire normally die from smoke or toxic-gas inhalation, and are dead before the flames consume their bodies.

Fire can be detected by fitting smoke alarms. They are inexpensive and providing the batteries are changed as instructed, will last for many years. Most have a test button, and some come with a built-in light indicator, and warning for those people with poor hearing. Do not be tempted to take the battery out just because you have overcooked the Sunday lunch and the kitchen is full of smoke.

Keeping a fire extinguisher in the kitchen for an emergency is always a good idea. They come filled with a variety of different contents, each extinguisher colour-coded and designed to react against a specific burning material. For example, a water-filled extinguisher will be red, and suitable for use on materials such as burning furniture – but will not be suitable for electrical fires. Make sure you choose the correct extinguisher for your home and are familiar with the operating instructions.

Routine fire checks

Many fires start through carelessness or forgetfulness. Make a routine before you go out, or before you go to bed at night. Check the house, especially where a potential fire hazard might exist.

➤ Make sure electrical sockets are not overloaded, especially in the kids' bedrooms. Wherever possible, use a bank of extension sockets that carry the British safety 'kite' mark

➤ Check that no clothes are left drying over electric or oil-fired heaters.

➤ Switch off and unplug electric appliances at night.

➤ Check that the cooker and oven are switched off properly.

➤ Extinguish any burning candles.

➤ Don't leave aerosol containers such as hairspray on top of hot surfaces.

➤ Don't build garden fires close to the house or wooden fences and sheds.

➤ Unplug electric blankets.

➤ Check out any burning smells and identify the source.

➤ Do not leave a smoking cigarette, even in an ashtray.

➤ Don't smoke when you have been drinking late at night.

➤ Don't smoke in bed, or when you feel tired.

Family fire drill

It is always a good idea to plan a simple fire drill with your family. Check over the house and look at all the doors and windows, imagine where a fire might start and make an escape plan accordingly.

➤ Show everyone how the smoke detectors work.

➤ Indicate where the fire extinguishers are located.

➤ Practice escape routes from different points of the house.

➤ Give individuals special tasks, e.g. to check on each other if in different bedrooms.

➤ Make someone responsible for the elderly or very young.

➤ Have an assembly point in a safe area outside, and check off everyone.

➤ Make sure everyone knows how to dial the emergency services and knows what to say.

LETTER BOMBS

The letter bomb has declined in use of late due to better detection devices in post offices and business premises. However, you should consider whether your lifestyle or occupation could make you a potential target in your home.

SUSPICIOUS PACKAGES

➤ Always be suspicious of unexpected packets or thick envelopes.

➤ Check any package that is heavier than you would expect for its size.

➤ Check any package that smells of almonds or marzipan.

➤ Check if grease appears to be leaking from the package.

➤ Do not bend or open any suspect package.

➤ Leave it undisturbed and vacate the room, locking the door behind you.

➤ Contact the police immediately.

NATURAL HAZARDS

Storms

Although Britain does not usually suffer from hurricanes, we do experience high winds and severe storms which can produce similar destruction to that of a hurricane. Wind speeds can reach over 100 mph during a violent storm, which has the effect of uprooting large trees and taking the roofs off some houses. Vehicles and people can be blown over in such winds. Whether you are abroad or at home, you should take every precaution to protect yourself during any type of violent storm:

➤ Take heed of early weather warnings.

➤ Put away any loose garden equipment or furniture: they can become dangerous missiles during the storm.

➤ Secure all doors and windows in your home and out-buildings.

➤ Check on any animals, and bring in any household pets.

➤ Put your car in the garage.

➤ Check on your supply of candles and torches,

➤ During violent storms or hurricanes, move into the cellar if available.

➤ Store drinking water in clean containers or the bath.

➤ Make sure your mobile phone is charged, as the telephone lines may come down.

➤ Keep your medical kit handy.

SAS ACTION

➤ In 1978 I was with a patrol that was part of a military operation in the United Arab Emirates. One day, while walking through the rough, dry, mountainous area, we stopped for the day and made camp in a dry wadi-bed. At around three in the afternoon the signaller received a message warning us of flash-floods. We thought that it had to be a joke: the heat in this rugged , mountainous desert was way up in the high 90s, so we ignored it. Some two hours later we all heard a strange noise, a kind of rumbling sound. Next thing, a wall of water about two feet high came rushing towards us. Luckily for us, we had made camp just a few feet above the wadi base, but still we were all forced to grab our kit and run like hell, clinging desperately to the earest rocky outcrop. It was not

(contd)

> the height of the water that was
> so dangerous, it was the force
> and the amount of debris that was
> being swept along. It would have
> taken the strongest swimmer down
> and crushed him.

Flooding

Flooding on a large scale is catastrophic and for this reason, the Thames Barrier was constructed to protect London, but in some parts of Britain, localised flooding happens on a regular basis. The effects of flooding isolate people and cause real damage problems. Floods can be anticipated and early flood warnings are given, normally over the local radio or, in more isolated areas, through a pre-arranged telephone network. People living near the sea, or close by a river flood plain are most at risk. If you know that the area in which you live is prone to flooding, check out the flood records at your local council office. Be prepared.

➤ Check fresh water and food supplies.

➤ Make sure all animals are taken to higher ground.

➤ Block doors with sandbags.

➤ Turn off mains electricity and gas. Boil all water, even that from the tap.

➤ As the water height increases, prepare to move upstairs.

➤ Flooding can arrive quite quickly, and stay for several days.

➤ Keep a mobile phone for real emergencies – rescue and help will be available.

➤ Do not resist if the authorities want you to evacuate.

➤ Beware of disease and possible hygiene threat due to flooded drains and sewers.

Emergency supply list

Many homes will automatically contain most of the items on this list, but it is worth checking through in advance of the time that you may need them.

➤ Tinned food for three days. If you are forced to cut the power, eat the contents of the deep freeze.

➤ Plastic eating and drinking utensils.

➤ Several plastic water containers. Water is for drinking only. Keep water purification tablets with your containers.

➤ Portable camping cookers and several gas bottles.

➤ Portable radio: the new wind-up type is perfect as it requires no batteries.

➤ Portable lights, torches and candles. Several disposable lighters.

➤ Large bucket with lid and plenty of toilet paper.

➤ First-air kit.

➤ Large, extra-strong bin bags.

Vehicle Safety

Car crime is not always random: it is normally done by youths who are looking for goods that they can exchange quickly for cash. In some cases, the youths are looking to use your car for joy-riding.

EVERYDAY PRECAUTIONS

Out of sight

From a security perspective, cars, like houses, have one major drawback: they have windows that can easily be broken to gain access. It is good advice never to leave any items of value exposed in your car. If it is not possible to take them with you, lock them in your boot.

Even when driving, avoid leaving your handbag or valuables on the front seat, or where they can be easily grabbed; there have been a spate of recent cases where women drivers have been targeted by thieves who have attacked their cars while stopped at traffic lights.

Service regularly

Most modern cars are very reliable, but if they are not treated with respect, they will break down. Many people often leave the servicing of their vehicle to the garage, and while this is a good thing, it is often helpful also to attend a short course on vehicle maintenance. Most local colleges and adult-learning centres offer such courses.

BASIC CHECKS

To make sure your car runs reliably, carry out the following checks on a weekly basis:

➤   Check your oil and water levels.

➤   Check that the pressure in all tyres is correct, not forgetting the spare.

➤   Check that you have all the correct equipment for changing a tyreand you know how to use it.

➤   Make sure the windscreen-washer bottle is kept filled up; during the winter, use a mix of water and anti-freeze.

If you break down

If your car breaks down, and you find yourself alone and in remote or unfamiliar surroundings, lock your doors and stay with the vehicle, particularly at night. A mobile phone is very useful in this situation. It is also a good idea to carry a medical kit in your car, not just for your own use but for others who may have had an accident.

In unfamiliar territory

Driving through unfamiliar streets, especially in rush-hour traffic, can be very confusing if you are not sure of your route and have no one to help you. Consider travelling outwith rush-hour times. Lock your doors and don't open them unless you are sure it's safe.

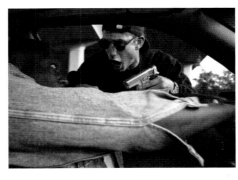

If someone tries to stop you, ignore them. If you come across the traffic-light car wash, and you can't dissuade him from washing your window by signals, wind your window down just a few inches and give them small change.

Remember, if you have to open the window, only open it a short way – never open it so than someone can get their hand inside and open the door. If you find yourself in a situation where someone tries to get into the car, and you cannot drive off, consider using a defensive weapon to beat back the arm. There are generally a good selection of weapons to have available, such as torches, screwdrivers or a heavy spanner (all legitimate tools to have in a car), and a can of de-icer will serve as a good deterrent spay. Keep them within easy reach of the driver's seat but if you use an improvised weapon, remember that you may be required to justify your actions with it.

Parking

If you park your car in a strange city, always put it in a car park with an attendant. Look for the security cameras, and park as close as possible within their vision, or if this isn't possible, choose a spot that is well lit.

If possible, never leave items in the car that will indicate your sex. Criminals will target women rather than men, so items such as handbags, toiletries or women's clothing left in the car will be a dead give-away.

When you return to your car, do so while the car park is still attended. Always have your keys ready to open the car. If you see a group of youths hanging around your car, seek assistance.

If, on returning to your car, you find that it has been broken into, stop and check the car. Bend down to see if anyone is underneath the vehicle and check through the back window to see if anyone is hiding inside.

SAS ACTION

➤ No matter where or when you park your car, always reverse into the spot. This should allow you to jump in the car and drive off without having to reverse, which is much slower.

Never be tempted to park in an unauthorised place. If your vehicle gets clamped, you can find yourself very vulnerable. If your car has been clamped, first read the instructions left by the clamping company, which will tell you where to go in order to pay your fine and get your car unclamped. Always take a taxi to the destination, and inquire how long it will be before they come to unclamp your car (it can take up to several hours). If your car is in a well-lit place, you may well be safe sitting in the locked car. Alternatively, find a nearby pub or café while you are waiting to be unclamped.

ROAD RAGE

Road rage is a relatively new phrase to describe a problem that has been around for some time. It arises mainly when drivers have no consideration for other road users. Confrontations normally arise when one driver does something to annoy another and in recent years such disputes have escalated into physical attacks where people have even been killed.

The following behaviour can help you avoid inciting road rage in others.

➤ Drive at a safe, steady speed.

➤ Give clear indications, in plenty of time, of your intentions, e.g. to turn left.

➤ Stay with the general flow of traffic.

➤ Stay in the correct lane on a motorway.

➤ Avoid being deliberately obstructive; e.g., let people into the flow of traffic from a side road.

➤ Avoid 'cutting up' other drivers .

Dealing with road rage

If you see another driver flashing their headlights at you, blowing their horn, or making gestures, don't automatically assume it's through road rage: first consider if they are justified in trying to tell you something. It is quite normal for other road users to indicate to you that something may be wrong with your car that you haven't noticed.

However, if you are being aggressively hassled by another driver:

➤ Smile and mouth the word 'sorry' if you have made a genuine mistake. This appeases most people.

Never get out of your car to confront someone as this often causes a tense situation to escalate into violence

➤ If they are in front of you, try to distance yourself from them by slowing down; otherwise maintain your speed.

➤ Avoid eye contact if the other driver draws alongside.

➤ Do not make obscene gestures, like giving the 'V' sign.

➤ Try to avoid stopping or being forced to stop by traffic lights, etc.

➤ Attacks can only occur when the vehicles have stopped and the drivers have confronted each other.

➤ If you do get caught in traffic, make sure all your doors are locked and the windows closed.

➤ Never get out of your car, unless you have been involved in an accident, and even then, stay very cool.

➤ If you find that someone is trying to get into you car, and it is not feasible to drive off because of heavy traffic, hit the horn and hold it down – they will soon lose interest.

VEHICLE BOMBS

Consider whether your lifestyle or occupation could make you a terrorist target. The vehicle bomb is normally fixed in place under the car, below the driver's seat. This is the easiest way of fixing a car bomb as it does not involve the terrorist having to get access below the bonnet. The only defence against such attacks is constant surveillance, and good personal security.

➤ Check your vehicle every time.

➤ Place a small strip of clear tape over the bonnet and boot, and check before you get in that it is still secure.

➤ Always lock your car and make sure the windows are fully closed.

➤ Check any sunroofs are secure.

➤ If possible, clear out your boot, glove compartment, etc.

➤ Mark the fixed position of your hub-caps with a felt pen.

Leave your car in a public, well-populated area, if possible. When returning to your car, go through the following procedure.

CAR BOMB CHECKLIST

➤ Search your vehicle without touching it.

➤ Check wheel arches, bumpes and spoilers.

➤ Get down on your knees and check below the vehicle

➤ Check for tape or wire.

➤ Check your security seals and marks

➤ Look for fingerprints on the bonnets, doors or boot

➤ Look through the window and check the interio

SAS ACTION

➤ Working in Northern Ireland required that I should check my vehicle several times a day. I found that it was best to keep my vehicle very dirty, as this helped to conceal the security tape placed on

(contd)

➤ it, and also helped to record finger
  marks if the car had been tampered
  with.

Travel

The last twenty years has seen a massive growth in the number of people who travel around the planet. A trip of any distance will usually involve flying, therefore you will visit an airport at least twice, and airports can be potentially dangerous places for the unwary traveller. While most flights are uneventful, arriving in a foreign country can pose a number of problems, enforced visa entry, taxation on foreign arrivals, searching your luggage and the confiscation of personal goods, and so on. Having cleared customs your next task is to get to your hotel safely; no problem get a taxi. This puts you in quite a vulnerable position, especially if you are visiting a place you have never been to before, and its not uncommon for people to pose as legitimate taxi drivers in order to rob tourists and in some cases murder them. Sounds unbelievable, just look in your daily newspaper. (See also Foreign Taxis, p.197.)

Western tourists are prime and obvious targets particularly in developing countries. Tourists can be literally ladened with valuable items – money, credit cards, passports, cameras, watches, even their clothes. How and where these items are removed from your person will depend on how well your protect yourself.

AIRPORTS

Your luggage is always at risk and the chances of it getting stolen are far greater at a Western airport. The most common form of theft involves distraction; one person will ask you the time while his accomplice makes off with your briefcase. Avoid this by doing the following.

Don't forget many countries ban the importation of some goods, such as weapons, alcohol and pornography. In the Middle East you can expect the customs to go through your luggage very carefully. What seems innocent to us in the West, such as a *Playboy* magazine, would certainly be confiscated in Saudi Arabia. If you travel to some African countries, don't be surprised if the customs seize items such as perfume and jewellery, in some cases it's the only way you can get into or out of the country. Whatever you do be patient and flexible with customs officers even if they are blatantly corrupt and downright annoying. However, if they look like taking you for a ride, complain in a loud voice about them being corrupt; it usually works, but on the other hand, you could find yourself being strip-searched.

➤ Stay with your luggage at all times.

➤ Get a trolley before you open the car boot and unload.

➤ Do not be distracted by strangers.

➤ Check in as quickly as possible.

➤ Hold onto your hand luggage at all times.

FOREIGN TAXIS

At most airports the taxi rank is well organised, but you will always get the odd driver who is not a member of the taxi rank touting for business just

inside the airport doors. Their favourite trick is to approach you and ask you your hotel name: 'Are you booked in at the Ampang Hotel?' To which being a stranger you reply, 'No, the Hilton'. With a flourish the man will turn and summon a friend who is waiting nearby: 'You need to go with this man for the Hilton.' In truth most of these guys are very convincing and you will normally finish up at your hotel, albeit in a rickety old car with a driver who thinks he's in a stock car race.

The best advice is to go to the official taxi stand with your trolley and buy a taxi ticket, you should then be shown together with your luggage to your transport. As an alternative you might e-mail the hotel and ask them to pick you up (most larger hotels offer an airport service), although some charge a small fee for this it is usually cheaper and safer than a taxi.

AUTHOR'S NOTE

➤ If you are alone in a South American country, never take a taxi outside the city. Its not just the cabbies that can take you for a ride, but many foreigners have disappeared into the jungle only to be found dead years later.

ACCOMMODATION

More than likely your travel arrangements will include your staying at a prearranged hotel; if they do not, always make sure you book accommodation beforehand. Those people who are back-packing are also advised to make prior arrangement. There are so many young people travelling today that most of the cheaper hostels are fully booked throughout the year. If you find yourself without accommodation, do

not sleep rough or wander the streets, use what money you have to book into a hotel for the night (see Money p.202). Sleeping rough is the one way to become parted from all you own. In a dire emergency go to a large hotel where you are likely to find other Westerners and seek help, most people will afford you the price of a meal and if your look genuine they may even pay for a room for the night. Americans and Europeans are particularly helpful, but be honest with them, show your passport and return flight ticket as evidence that you are not just on the make.

Your suitcase will normally be fairly safe until you pick it up at your destination airport and from then on it will remain in your hotel or accommodation. The whole idea of a holiday is to be free to observe the sights and travel around. The country you visit will depend on how secure your luggage is. Choosing a good hotel should ensure you come back to a clean change of clothing, but if you are not taking any valuable items on the sight-seeing trips make sure they are locked away with hotel security. Place the camera strap around your neck as it can easily be pulled from your shoulder. Take only the money you require for the day and only carry one credit card.

CITIES AND YOUNG TRAVELLERS

If you are on holiday in a strange city, or in a foreign country, with your children try to stay together. Many cities especially in the Far East are bustling with people and it is easy to get separated in large crowds, or at busy commuter terminals. Depending on the age of the children, I have found it beneficial to play a little game. As you move from place to place, have the children suggest some prominent location, which they know they can find – a McDonald's restaurant, for example. Choose a new location about every two hundred metres or so, this way if you get separated, they will always have a rendezvous point.

Don't walk about a strange city unless you are in an area known to be safe. If the neighbourhood looks dodgy, take a cab from place to place. Make sure you always take a proper licensed taxi.

WHEN ABROAD

➤ Remember that most people are basically good.

➤ Smile disarmingly – be modest.

➤ Do not put people down, just because they have a different culture.

➤ Dress yourself to obey their laws and customs, walking through an Arab market in a bikini, while the faithful are being called to prayer is not advisable

BARS AND SEX

Many cities have developed a culture where alcohol, drugs and sex are the prime means for extracting money from visitors. London, Amsterdam, Las Vegas, Rio de Janeiro, and Bangkok to mention but a few. In some countries these activities are closely monitored by the authorities while in others anything goes providing you have the money.

However, the risk of infection through having unprotected sex is extremely high. Most prostitutes, both male and female, are infected with one or more diseases. In addition the establishments that offer such services also offer alcohol and drugs which confuse the mind and leave you at risk not just to disease but also to mugging or worse.

While some sexual diseases cause little more than personal embarrassment others can be life-threatening. Even when protection against sexual disease is worn a prostitute can still transmit infection through kissing, open sores and body lice.

AIDS

Many prostitutes are infected with the HIV virus, especially in Africa where AIDS is an enormous problem. The risk of infectionwill depend on the individual factors involved, but this is still something to keep in mind when travelling in any country with a high occurrence of AIDS.

MONEY

In many of the less-developed countries Westerners are often seen as purely a source of easy money. It is always best, therefore, when you are out sightseeing or whatever to carry the minimum amount of cash you will need and to consider if you need to take any credit cards at all.

KEEP YOUR MONEY SAFE

➤ Only carry what you need for the day - leave the rest in a secure place such as the hotel safe.

➤ Consider wearing a hidden money belt.

➤ In a high risk area, carry a dummy wallet with just a small amount of money in it. Throw this at the muggers then run away.

➤ Make use of traveller's cheques, as they can be easily replaced.

➤ Always carry the telephone numbers for reporting lost credit cards, traveller's cheques, etc.

➤ Insure your credit cards against loss and misuse.

In the worst-case scenario you need to be able to exit a country or get to a safe haven quickly, and this can only be done with money. While insurance is a good idea, it can in some cases prove to be slow and cumbersome, especially if civil war has broken out. Always carry at least several large denomination US dollars (accepted everywhere) and one major credit card. Secrete these about you person where they will not be found, such as the lining of your clothing.

MOBILE PHONES

If you are a young adventurer with little or no experience of foreign travel take a GSM mobile phone with you. These should be kept with a fully charged battery ready for any real emergency. When confronted with a serious problem others, such as your friends and parents, will be able to help if they know of your plight. Providing that you only intend to use your mobile phone for emergencies, the cost is not too great. Anyway, the advantages of having one far outweigh the costs.

AUTHOR'S NOTE

➤ I once paid out around £85 per month to a prominent British insurance company, a precaution undertaken through media advertising for worldwide travel. In the event when I became ill in at a hotel in Malaysia I asked for a doctor. The insurance company declined any help saying my policy did not cover such an emergency. I finished up paying $70 US dollars for a visit and medication. So be sure to read through any policy very carefully before taking it out.

WOMEN TRAVELLERS

In certain parts of the world Western women are thought to be promiscuous. This attitude if further compounded in those countries which also view women in general as second-class citizens. If a lone Western woman does not respect the traditions of such a country, particularly in the way she dresses, she may well find herself harassed and in some cases imprisoned.

If you find yourself being hassled it usually will be by younger men. Most imagine that you, as a Western woman, are easy prey to their advances. If you are seriously accosted, look for a help from a policeman or older men who might be near by. Unless you are sure, do not venture out alone on the streets at night, as you can be taken for a prostitute. Trust your instincts and stay within a group if you want to stay out to the early hours.

Despite what I have written above I firmly believe that if you obey the local law and traditions you will come to no harm. Rape does happen, but it's not very common - in fact it's more likely to happen in a Western country.

PUBLIC TRANSPORT

If you intend staying out late, consider booking a taxi in advance. If you are a woman travelling by yourself, you might request a woman driver. Sit behind the driver, if your driver gets funny or tries to take

advantage of you, ask him to stop at a well-lit area, or where there are plenty of people.

Tubes and buses can be dangerous places at night. Tr to stay away from isolated bus stops. On an empty bus sit near a driver, on the tube sit near an exit with the alarm. If you see several hooligans or drunks getting on, consider if you are best getting off at the next safest stop. Waiting a few minutes for the next tube could be a wise move.

Trains running in the late evening often become emptier as they progress along their route. If you should find yourself in an empty compartment, move to a carriage where there are more passengers.

HITCH-HIKING

Hitch-hiking is not as safe as it was. If your only method of travel depends on getting a lift consider the following guidelines:

➤ Do not get into a vehicle with just one person. Choose a family if possible.

➤ Arrange your lift at a well-lit service station, watch people coming or leaving and ask their destination.

➤ Offer to pay your way if you have money.

➤ Make sure other people see you getting a lift.

➤ Do not get dropped off in an isolated area.

➤ If you are unsure, stay in a service area, and ring family or friends.

➤ If you are distressed, ring the local police or British Consulate.

TRAVEL DISEASES

Drinking water or eating food that has been contaminated, usually with infected human and animal faeces or urine, is the general cause for diarrhoeal-type illnesses. In many isolated and tropical countries people are less discriminate where they defecate and these germs eventually find their way into the local water supply or are carried to the food by flies.

Locally prepared drinks, milk, ice and ice-cream should all be treated as suspect, because they are only as pure as the water they are made from. This is particularly so in the tropical countries where the local ice-cream is a mixture of crushed ice and flavouring.

AUTHOR'S NOTE

➤ Do not be put off by the sight of street
vendors selling food - just check that they
are being hygienic. In many cases I have
found the food on the streets to be far better
and safer than that in the hotels.

Diarrhoea

Most people who travel to a foreign land will suffer
from bouts of continuous diarrhoea. Although
unpleasant they pose no threat to life and the
disorder is usually self-limiting. In the case of the
average traveller, the cause is usually untraceable. You
are probably suffering from diarrhoea if the number
of daily bowel movements are increased by a factor of
two or more, with stools being squishy and watery.
Nausea and vomiting are frequently caused by
infections of the stomach or intestines. Many times
these are viral so that antibiotics are of no value.
These infections will usually resolve without treatment
in 24 to 48 hours.

Treatment

The most important thing is avoid dehydration. Water
loss must be replaced using sterile water (boiled or

bottled) mixed with a little salt. Check out the local pharmacies for electrolyte powders. A juice made from potassium-rich fruit such as apples and oranges will also help, as will honey if it can be found.

Dysentery

Dysentery is an infection of the colon caused by bacteria or amoeba. The diarrhoea is painful with the stools containing blood and mucus. Bacillary dysentery is normally found in tropical and sub-tropical countries where amoebic dysentery is a najor problem. In general, both are caused by poor personal hygiene in the preparation or handling of food. Flies also spread the infection, and some infected people can act as carriers while showing no signs of having the disease.

The symptoms of bacillary dysentery can appear anywhere from 30 minutes to 12 hours after consuming contaminated food. They range from mild stomach upset with loose stools to the rapid onset of rigorous and painful cramps with acute bloody diarrhoea. Although the casualty may also suffer nausea, vomiting is rare. Some of the more severe cases can be mistaken for other gastric or intestinal disorders.

Amoebic dysentery is much rarer and the onset and symptoms sometimes takes three or four weeks to develop. The stools are foul-smelling and stained with blood – there is a lot of straining.

Treatment

As with any infection treatment will depend on the severity, but most dysentery symptoms will disappear within 24 to 36 hours. Mild cases can be treated with kaolin while the more serious cases of bacillary dysentery will need antibiotic treatment. The need to replace body fluid and salt is essential.

DRUGS

Dealing with a Drug User

When confronted with a person who you believe to be high on drugs you must decide which avenue you want to take. This decision can be made in a few seconds during which time you should try to assess the physical condition of your assailant. If they are staggering, rolling their head in order to maintain their focus and slurring their words, you should consider running for it. Most drugs affect the respiratory system making running at speed difficult. If, on the other hand, your assailant is hyperactive the

chances are they have taken amphetamines, which help to speed up the responses and unless you are very fit your chances of getting away are less likely. However, you can probably confuse the assailant by throwing down your dummy wallet and this might give you time to escape.

Drug Dealers

Beware the false friend; never take parcels or packages back home for people who claim to have friends in the UK. If you are caught trying to slip two kilos of cocaine through customs, you can end up on death row in some countries. Drug dealers and traffickers can be very persuasive, either through feigning friendship, money or threats. If you are confronted by such a character, play along until you can extract yourself without undue attention.

UNWANTED FRIENDS

At one time or another we all get stuck with the unwanted friend. The majority of these often appear in the seat next to you on the aircraft, which means at least you can fall asleep in the knowledge that when the aircraft lands you will be rid of them. Being picked-up by an unwanted friend in another country is a different matter. While there are those that make a beeline for men, the majority go for a woman on her own.

➤ If you get into conversation always start the dialogue with the fact that you must be back at your hotel in 10 minutes. This gives you time to make an assessment of your new friend, and so if you wish to part company you have made your excuse before hand.

➤ Never tell anyone the name of your hotel.

➤ Don't take your room key out with you not only does it give away the name of your hotel, it can also be stolen leaving you to return to a ransacked room.

➤ Not all strangers are drug-crazed scruffs in jeans and a torn T-shirt. Many drugs dealers dress and behave in an impeccable manner.

➤ Don't fall in love with the first handsome or beautiful stranger that promises to show you the city and all its delights.

Medical Emergencies

The subject of first aid is vast, and so the methods mentioned here are designed to deal primarily with injuries resulting from fights or attacks. It may be that you were not involved in the actual conflict, but it would be wrong of anyone not to assist an injured person. However, a word of caution about doing so: if the injured party is drunk and being uncooperative, seek assistance, and if they become violent, leave them alone. In these circumstances, they are likely to do more harm to themselves – or to you – if you try to persevere.

In many assault situations, personal injury may have been sustained by one or more people. Once the need for first aid has been assessed, priorities should be established when dealing with several casualties. The situation itself will impose its own directions. Whatever the circumstances, keep these general rules in mind:

MEDICAL EMERGENCIES

➤ Keep calm. However serious an injury or dangerous a

situation, panic will impair your ability to think clearly and so lower your effectiveness.

➤ Do not waste time – time can mean life or death.

➤ Avoid any unnecessary danger to yourself. This is not cowardice. You will be no help to anybody if you suffer needless injury.

➤ Think carefully, but quickly, before you act.

➤ Do your best to reassure and comfort any casualty.

➤ Ask others to help you deal with the situation, in particular anyone with medical qualifications or experience.

PRIORITIES

When assessing individual casualties, use your own senses to the full:

➤ Ask.

➤ Look.

➤ Listen.

➤ Smell.

➤ Then think and act.

In emergency situations, the following concerns always take priority:

➤ that the casualty has a clear airway.

➤ that they are able to breathe.

➤ that they have a pulse, with no arterial bleeding.

➤ that neck injuries are not moved.

If the casualty is conscious, airway and breathing checks are not so vital, so check first – speak to the casualty. Ask them to describe their symptoms and get them to tell you what they think is wrong.

Airway

With the casualty on his back and unconscious, his airway may be blocked by a foreign body – such as vomit or dentures – or by a constriction of the air passage, caused by

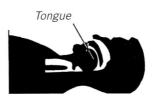

Tongue

unconsciousness or the position of his head which has caused his tongue to fall back inside the mouth. To check, listen with your ear close to his mouth whilst looking at his chest. If you cannot detect any sound or chest movement, you must act to ensure that the airway is clear:

➤ Press down on the forehead whilst gently lifting under the neck.

➤ Keeping one hand on the forehead, push the chin gently upwards – this will dislodge the tongue.

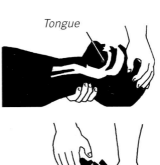

Tongue

Listen for breathing again at this point.

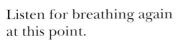

215

➤ If there are still no signs of breathing, turn the head to one side and use two fingers to sweep any debris from the mouth. Be careful not to push any matter further into the throat.

➤ Turn the head back to the normal position and listen for breathing again.

Breathing

If at any time the casualty starts breathing again, put them in the recovery position. If the breathing is heavy or noisy, check again for any remaining blockage in the mouth.

If there are still no signs of breathing after completing the above checks, the problem may be with the casualty's circulation, that is, the heart has stopped pumping blood around the body. Firstly, however, you must breathe for the patient (irrespective of pulse), as explained in the section on CPR (see p.217).

Circulation

Checking the casualty's pulse will determine whether the heart is still beating. This can be done in either of the following ways:

➤ Using the tips of two fingers, gently slide them down the side of the casualty's Adam's apple towards the back of the neck until you feel a soft groove. Press gently on this spot.

➤ Rest your fingers lightly on the front of the wrist,

about 1 cm back from the wrist joint on the thumb side (close to where a watchstrap would normally fasten).

If there is a pulse, place the casualty in the recovery position (see p.220). If you cannot feel a pulse, help is needed urgently.

ACT IMMEDIATELY

If you can't get the casualty breathing or there is no sign of a pulse, then you must act immediately. Without breathing or circulating blood, oxygen cannot get to the brain which will begin to sustain damage after only three minutes. If you have help at hand, send someone to phone the emergency services. If you are alone and cannot summon help within 30 seconds, you must attend to the injured yourself.

CARDIOPULMONARY RESUSCITATION (CPR)

CPR is the preferred method of reviving someone who has stopped breathing or whose heart has stopped beating. There are two components to this procedure, one involving assisted ventilations to restore breathing, the other involving chest compression to restart the heart.

WARNING

➤ NEVER give compression if the heart is beating or if only a faint pulse can be felt – it could stop the heart.

CPR techniques are as follows:

➤ Position yourself to the side of the casualty's chest.

➤ Extend the neck by tilting the head well back, as in the airway check (see p.215)

➤ Hold the jaw well open and close the nostrils by pinching them with your fingers (pic. 1 below).

➤ Seal the casualty's mouth with yours – a handkerchief may be used as a filter – and blow steadily until you can see his chest rising (pic. 2).

➤ Do this 4 times and then check for breathing. Whether breathing or not, re-check the pulse. If there is one and the patient is now breathing, then use the recovery position.

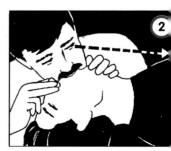

Note: if the casualty's mouth is injured and cannot be used for ventilations, the nostrils can be used instead.

Seal the mouth with your thumb, put your mouth over the nostrils and proceed as described above. Breathing will not restart without a pulse and if at this point, there is still no pulse, you must compress the chest in the following manner:

➤ From the same position, place your interlocked hands in the middle of the casualty's chest (pic.3).

➤ With straight arms, held as vertically as possible, press quickly 15 times, with half-a-second between each compression. Do not press too hard – enough pressure to depress the chest 2–5 cm will suffice.

➤ Follow this with a further 2 ventilations in the manner described above.

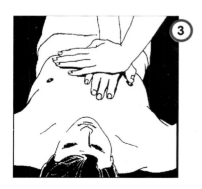
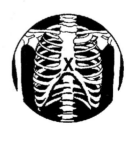

Contine this combination of compressions and ventilation until help arrives.

CPR compression/ventilation ratios

If you have help

With two or more people dealing with the injured, two people should carry out the CPR, one person dealing with each of the tasks.

➤ Aim to establish a routine of 5 compressions followed by 1 ventilation, continuing in cycles.

If there are only two people dealing with the casualties, send one for help first before getting them to assist you with the CPR

If you are alone

➤ Aim to establish a routine of 15 compressions to 2 ventilations. Take a further pulse/breathing check after 4 cycles and then after every 3 minutes. If a pulse recurs, continue ventilations alone until the casualty breathes for himself.

If breathing and pulse restart before expert help arrives, place the casualty in the recovery position (see opposite). This however is unlikely to happen, so continue with the CPR until it does.

THE RECOVERY POSITION

Generally, an unconscious person who is breathing and who has a reasonable heartbeat, and is without other injuries demanding immediate attention should be put into the recovery (or coma) position. This position is the safest because it minimises the risk of

impeded breathing. The tilted-back head ensures open air passages. The face-down attitude allows any vomit or other liquid obstruction to drain from the mouth. The spread of the limbs will maintain the body in its position. If fractures or other injuries prevent suitable placing of the limbs, use rolled clothing or other padded objects to prop the injured in this position.

WARNING

Do not use the recovery position if:

➤ the casualty has a suspected spinal injury.

➤ the casualty is not unconscious or is unlikely to become so.

Placing a casualty in the recovery position

➤ Kneel to one side of the casualty with their arms by their side.

➤ Gently pull the casualty over and towards you, by grasping their clothing at the hip.

➤ Move the arm and leg on one side outwards, bending the elbow and knee as shown in the diagram, to stop the patient lying flat.

➤ Keep the other arm straight and close to the casualty's side.

➤ Turn the head in the direction of the bent arm.

➤ Position the head slightly back to ensure the casualty has a clear airway

➤ Check the airway is clear and do not leave the casualty unattended.

CHOKING

Any person showing serious signs of choking is in need of immediate assistance. These may include:

➤ the casualty being unable to speak or breathe.

➤ the skin going pale blue.

➤ the casualty grasping their throat.

The condition is usually caused by something lodged in the windpipe which prevents free passage of air to the lungs.

Action

Removal of the obstruction is an urgent requirement. A conscious person should be encouraged to cough it away. If this is ineffective, check inside the mouth to see if the blockage can be cleared by a finger. If the choking continues, gravity and slapping should be tried to shake it free.

➤ Help the casualty to bend forward so that the head is below lung level.

➤ Slap the person sharply between the shoulder blades, using the heel of the hand. This may be repeated three more times if necessary.

➤ Check inside the mouth and remove the obstruction if it has been freed.

➤ If it has not, try to clear it using air pressure generated abdominal thrusts.

Abdominal thrusts

If the casualty is conscious and upright:

➤ Stand behind him and put your arms around his waist.

➤ Clench one fist and place it with thumb side against his abdomen. Make sure it is resting between his naval and the lower end of the breastbone.

➤ Place your other hand over the fist.

➤ Make a firm thrust backwards and into the abdomen. Do this up to four times if required. Pause after each thrust and be prepared to remove anything dislodged from the air passage.

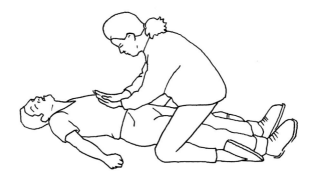

Should the choking still persist, repeat the four back slaps and the four abdominal thrusts alternately until the obstruction is cleared.

If an unconscious casualty requires abdominal thrusts

➤   Turn the casualty on his back.

➤   Kneeling astride him, place the heel of one hand between the navel and breastbone, and put the other hand on top.

➤   Deliver the four thrusts as above.

If the obstruction persists, and the patient stops breathing, begin assisted breathing and chest compression as described above.

BLEEDING

In fights and assaults where a weapon has been used,

or someone has taken a heavy beating, there will be a fair amount of bleeding. Bleeding should be stopped as soon as possible, but remember that checks for response, airway, breathing and circulation ALWAYS come first. There are three options available: direct and indirect pressure, and elevation.

Direct pressure and elevation

The object of this treatment is to slow down or stop the loss of blood until the body's own defences come into play. The blood will clot relatively quickly if the flow is slowed or stopped, and although a cleanly cut blood vessel may bleed profusely if left untreated, it will tend to shrink, close and retreat into its surrounding tissue. Sometimes these natural methods will succeed in arresting bleeding entirely unaided.

Pressure

➤ Place a dressing over the wound and apply firm but gentle pressure with the hand. A sterile dressing is desirable. If one is not available, any piece of clean cloth can be used.

➤ If no dressing is ready for immediate use, cover the wound with your hand. If necessary, hold the edges of the wound together with gentle pressure. Any dressings used should be large enough to overlap the wound and cover the surrounding area.

➤ If blood comes through the first dressing, apply a second over the first, and if required, a third over the second.

➤ Keep even pressure applied by tying on a firm bandage. Take great care that the bandage is not so tight that, like a tourniquet, it restricts the flow of blood.

Large wounds

If the wound is large and suitable dressings are to hand, bring the edges of the wound together and use the dressings to keep the wound closed. To arrest the flow of blood from a very large wound, make a pad of the dressing and press it into the wound where the bleeding is heaviest. If there is any sharp or protruding debris in the wound, pad around it and leave it in place.

Reassurance and rest play their vital part in the treatment since they can lower the rate of heartbeat and so reduce the flow of blood around the body. The patient should therefore be lying down while being treated.

Elevation

If there is no danger of any other injury being aggravated, an injured limb is best raised as high as is comfortable for the casualty. This reduces the blood flow in the limb, helps the veins to drain the area and so assists in reducing the blood loss through the wound. This should be done before any bandaging is done.

Indirect pressure

If a combination of these procedures does not

succeed, the use of appropriate pressure points must be considered. It is necessary to recognise the type of external bleeding, because pressure points can only be used to control arterial bleeding.

TYPES OF BLEEDING

➤ Blood from the arteries is bright red and spurts out in time with each heartbeat

➤ Blood from the veins is darker red, with less pressure and flows out steadily

A place where an artery runs across a bone near the surface of the skin constitutes a pressure point. There are a variety of pressure points which can be used to control heavy arterial bleeding, depending on the site of the wound.

For wounds

➤ on the temple or scalp: forward of or above the ear (pic. 1 overleaf);

➤ on the face below the eyes: the side of the jaw (pic. 2);

➤ on the shoulder or upper arm: above the clavicle (collar bone) (pic. 3);

➤ on the elbow: the underside of the upper arm (pic. 4);

➤ on the lower arm: the inside flex of the elbow (pic. 5);

➤ on the hand: the front of the wrist (pic. 6);

➤ on the thigh: midway between the groin and the top of the thigh (pic. 7);

➤ on the lower leg: the upper sides of the knee (pic. 8);

➤ on the foot: the front of the ankle (pic. 9)

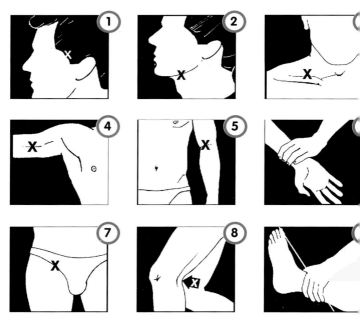

When using pressure points to control bleeding, make full use of the opportunity to dress the wound more effectively.

Pressure-application technique

The technique to use when applying pressure to arteries is:

➤ With the casualty lying down, locate the fingers or thumb over the pressure point and apply sufficient pressure to flatten the artery and arrest the flow of blood.

➤ Re-dress the wound.

➤ Maintain the pressure for at least 10 minutes to allow time for blood-clotting to begin. **Do not exceed 15 minutes** or the tissues below the pressure point will begin to be damaged by the deprivation of arterial blood. It is essential to release the controlling pressure after 15 minutes.

SELF-HELP

Try to prepare mentally for the unlikely – but possible – moment when you may yourself be injured, conscious and alone. Try to have ready a self-help routine, such as the following.

➤ Lie down and rest – in a sheltered spot if possible.

➤ Apply direct pressure to your wound. Put a dressing, improvised or otherwise, on it.

➤ Tie on a bandage tightly enough to maintain firm pressure without restricting circulation.

➤ Elevate the injury if possible. Keep as still as possible to relieve pain.

SHOCK

Shock is a condition resulting from either illness or injury, which reduces the volume of blood or fluid, causing weakness to the body. Often referred to as traumatic or injury shock, it is a serious condition which can be fatal, even after bodily injuries have been treated. Extreme cases of pain or fear can also produce shock symptoms although this is usually self-correcting .

CAUSES OF SHOCK

The causes of shock from blood or fluid loss are as follows:

➤ Blood loss from either external or internal bleeding.

➤ Loss of plasma from severe burns.

➤ Heart attack.

➤ Loss of water from intestinal blockage.

➤ Recurrent vomiting.

➤ Severe diarrhoea.

➤ Dehydration.

Symptoms of shock:

➤ The person will be weak, feel faint, possibly at the same time being restless and anxious.

➤ There may be a feeling of sickness or a need to vomit.

➤ The person will be thirsty.

➤ The skin becomes cold, clammy and pale, with possible sweating.

➤ The person may yawn or sigh, with shallow, rapid breathing.

➤ The pulse will increase but also become weaker and sometimes irregular, due to blood and fluid loss. It may disappear altogether at the wrist.

➤ Unconsciousness will occur if left untreated.

Treatment of shock

Generally, shock requires fluid replacement and therefore, expert help. You can assist by:

➤ Lying the patient down and possibly raising the legs slightly (injuries permitting).

➤ Dress all wounds (as outlined above).

➤ Keep the casualty warm and comfortable, reducing all movement and pain if possible.

➤ Watch for loss of response.

➤ Allow small sips of water only, if the patient is conscious.

CARDIAC ARREST

It only takes 15–30 seconds to lose consciousness after the heart stops, due to lack of oxygen to the brain after the blood pressure drops to zero. You may also encounter muscular spasms like those of a fit, and vomiting.

Why the heart stops beating

Ventricular fibrillation and vagal inhibition are two reasons for the heart to stop beating.

Vagal inhibition

One of the vagus nerve's functions is to control the heart rate. It controls the heart by keeping it beating at approximately 60 beats per minute when at rest and adjusts itself for other activities, such as exercise. Over-stimulation of the nerve can either slow the heart considerably or stop it altogether.

Shock – either a physical pain or a nasty fright, pressure on a certain part of the neck, or kicking or punching the front lower chest can all cause abnormal function of the vagus nerve.

A punch or kick to the chest, or hitting a certain part of the neck are most likely to happen in a fight. This can be very serious and if a person does lose consciousness in these types of circumstances, it is vital to check their airway, breathing and circulation immediately.

Ventricular fibrillation

Ventricular fibrillation occurs when the ventricles of the heart start contracting at a rate of over 400 times per minute due to an irritable heart muscle. At this speed the ventricles cannot fill with blood and so the blood stops circulating. After three to four minutes, death will occur because the brain stops functioning. There is no pulse as the patient will be unconscious. An irritable heart muscle is often the result of angina or a previous heart attack. An angina attack can sometimes be a warning sign, so if a person is exercising and suffers such an atttack, they must rest immediately.

When a cardiac arrest happens you have no time to waste. Once the heart has stopped beating you only have two minutes before irreversible brain damage occurs unless you can restore the blood circulation to the brain. After four minutes the heart will never start again. So it is vital to think quickly, stay calm and start resuscitation immediately. Only expert help can resolve the situation so do not delay in summoning help.

FRACTURES

Fractures are the most common injuries to bones. If excessive force is applied to a bone this can result in a discontinuity in the cortex, resulting in either a complete break in a major bone or a more minor injury.

A more serious fracture is normally caused by a direct hit; for example, falling onto a hard object or being kicked, or even by falling and bending the bone in an outstretched hand. Serious fractures can occur when people jump off walls or over fences and do not land correctly. If you were to land on your heels while keeping your knees straight you could not only create a direct fracture in your heel but could also fracture your thigh-bone; and in more serious cases fracture the base of the skull, as the force of the landing can be transmitted through your body.

SIGNS OF BONE FRACTURE

A bone fracture should be suspected if any or all of the following signs are present:

➤ Difficulty in normal movement of any part of the body.

➤ Pain around the injured area.

➤ Swelling or bruising accompanied by tenderness in the area of the injury.

➤ Deformity or shortening of the injured part.

➤ Grating of bone heard during examination or attempted movement.

➤ Signs of shock.

➤ The injured having heard or felt a bone break.

➤ Loss of power in the injured limb.

Diagnosis of fractures

It is important to find out as many details about how the person has been injured – the more you know, the easier it is to decide if you think there is a fracture, and where to look for it.

Signs to look for are:

➤ Tenderness and swelling.

➤ Loss of movement in joints above and below the fracture.

➤ Any deformity in a limb when compared to the one on the other side.

A further sign of a fracture is a condition known as crepitus where the broken ends of the bone rub together, causing a grating sensation. Do not set out to look for this sign, as your investigations will only cause more pain and do more harm than good.

Types of fracture

There are two basic types of fracture:

➤ Closed fractures.

➤ Open fractures.

Closed fracture

In a closed fracture, there is no break in the skin at the point of fracture. Irrespective of the degree of fracture, the same principles of treatment apply:

➤ Immobilisation;

➤ Support.

The fractured limb should be supported and tied (not too tightly – check pulses below the site of the injury to ensure blood flow) in the position it is found.

Movement of the affected area should never be attempted. If you unsure whether the area is fractured or sprained, assume the worst and treat as a fracture.

Open fractures

An open fracture is one where the bone has, or is still, protruding through the skin. A wound points to the site of the fracture. This is always a serious injury, as blood loss and infection usually occur.

Treat as for a closed fracture, but lightly dressing the wound (be sure to avoid applying pressure to it when placing the dressing).

Common fractures

Skull fractures

The purpose of the skull is to provide a strong, protective 'shell' for the brain. Damage to the skull bone may not necessarily be evident; there may be a depressed fracture or a leakage of blood from the fracture could cause pressure to the brain itself.

All head injuries must be regarded as serious, even if there is no noticeable wound. They can cause brain damage, or loss of consciousness, which could mask other conditions. A direct blow to the head or a fall would cause a fracture to the cranium (the crown of the head). A blow to the jaw or an indirect force, such as landing hard on your feet from a high jump, may cause a fracture to the base of the skull.

SYMPTOMS OF SKULL FRACTURES

➤ Obvious injuries to the head.

➤ Blood or clear, watery cerebrospinal fluid emitted from the ear or nose.

➤ The pupils of the eyes may be unequal.

➤ Bloodshot eyes, turning to black (bruising) later.

➤ Lapsing into unconsciousness.

Concussion: if any of the above symptoms are present then concussion or a skull fracture should be suspected.

If the casualty is unconscious, their breathing and pulse should be monitored. If they are present, the injured should be placed in the recovery position.
If conscious, place them in a reclining position with head and shoulders supported. Keep the injured warm and handle them gently.

Collar-bone fractures

Fractures to the collar-bone are rarely due to a direct blow. They are more usually caused by an indirect force, such as a fall on to the point of the shoulder or an outstretched hand.

SYMPTOMS OF COLLAR
BONE FRACTURES

➤ General signs of fracture.

➤ Swelling visible or felt at the site of the fracture.

➤ Pain at the fracture point is increased by movement.

➤ Reluctance of the injured person to move the arm on the side of the injury.

➤ Attempts by the injured person to relieve pain by supporting the injured side by holding the elbow and keeping their head inclined towards the injury.

Arm fractures

The bones most commonly broken are the wrist bones, although there can be fractures at any point of the two forearm bones or the upper arm, and quite possibly the elbow.

SYMPTOMS OF ARM FRACTURES

➤ General signs of fracture.

➤ Pain at the fracture point is increased by movement.

➤　Inability of the injured to use the injured arm.

➤　If there is an elbow fracture, it will be impossible to bend it – do not try.

Splints

Splints can be improvised from just about anything – even a tight roll of clothing or bedding. Pad the splint and fasten it so that it supports the joints above and below the fracture. A fractured leg can be partially immobilised by tying it to the good leg if nothing else is available. A fractured leg may be deformed, shortened, or twisted unnaturally.

Re-alignment of limbs

In cases where there is a long delay before professional medical assistance, re-alignment of a limb should be attempted before immobilisation, but only if there is no pulse below the fracture and the skin is white and pallid. This is a potentially dangerous manoeuvre and should never be attempted unless these conditions are present. Carefully pull the end of the limb until a pulse re-appears below the site of the injury, and then splint it in that position.

The only further help that can be given is to keep the patient warm and comfortable and checking the airway, breathing and circulation. If the casualty loses consciousness, you may have to use the recovery position regardless of the fracture.raise the injured part to cut down swelling and discomfort, and to treat any symptoms of shock. The casualty then needs rest.